Xamarin Cross-platform Application Development

Develop production-ready applications for iOS and Android using Xamarin

Jonathan Peppers

PUBLISHING

BIRMINGHAM - MUMBAI

Xamarin Cross-platform Application Development

First published: February 2014

Production Reference: 1060214

Published by Packt Publishing Ltd.
Livery Place
35 Livery Street
Birmingham B3 2PB, UK.

ISBN 978-1-84969-846-7

www.packtpub.com

Cover Image by Yuvraj Mannari (yuvrajm@packtpub.com)

Credits

Author

Jonathan Peppers

Reviewers

Pierce Boggan

Betim Drenica

Tom Opgenorth

William Thomas

Acquisition Editors

Sam Birch

Richard Harvey

Content Development Editor

Neeshma Ramakrishnan

Technical Editors

Tanuj Gulati

Adrian Raposo

Copy Editors

Dipti Kapadia

Kirti Pai

Project Coordinator

Kranti Berde

Proofreaders

Simran Bhogal

Ameesha Green

Indexers

Hemangini Bari

Tejal Soni

Graphics

Ronak Dhruv

Abhinash Sahu

Production Coordinator

Nilesh Bambardekar

Cover Work

Nilesh Bambardekar

About the Author

Jonathan Peppers is a Xamarin MVP and the lead developer of the popular cross-platform game, Draw a Stickman: EPIC. Jon works for Hitcents, a software development company based in Bowling Green, Kentucky. He has been working with the C# programming language for over 7 years. He has also been working with technologies such as WinForms, WPF, ASP.NET WebForms, and ASP.NET MVC. In recent years, Hitcents has been heavily investing in mobile development with Xamarin and has developed nearly 40 mobile applications across multiple platforms.

About the Reviewers

Pierce Boggan is a student of Software Engineering at the Auburn University. He has a passion for software, entrepreneurship, and theology. In the past, Pierce has worked for Xamarin as a Customer Support Engineering Intern. He also hosts a bi-monthly podcast with Chris Hardy in which all things related to Xamarin and mobile development are discussed. You can find him blogging about software, specifically mobile development, at www.pierceboggan.com.

> I would like to thank my Lord and Savior Jesus Christ, as well as my close friends and family who have supported me along the way.

Betim Drenica is a professional developer with over a decade's experience and has specialized in many technologies from database to client technologies to mobiles. He considers himself as a software architect oriented in Service Oriented Applications (RESTing for a long time) paying more attention to mobile apps for all major platforms (Windows Phone, Android, and iOS) using Xamarin. Being a very community-driven person, he is the founder and leader of two user groups, Albanian SQL Server UG and Albanian .NET UG. He is a Microsoft Certified Trainer and a regular speaker at many tech conferences. He's a blogger and you can find him at www.betimdrenica.wordpress.com and usually tweets from time to time on his Twitter account @betimdrenica. He also spends a good amount of his time on LinkedIn at http://www.linkedin.com/in/betim.

Tom Opgenorth is an IT professional from Alberta, Canada. His interest in computing started in 1983 when he taught himself Applesoft Basic and steadily progressed from there on. For the past 20 years, he has taken on many roles in IT, such as developer/engineer, QA, team lead, and architect. Tom settled on the .NET platform in 2002 with an interest in C#, and became a fan of Mono in 2003. He was awarded the Microsoft MVP award for C# in 2008, 2009, and 2010. In early 2008, he purchased his first smartphone, the Android Developer Phone 1, and has been hooked on mobile technologies with a focus on Android ever since.

Tom is currently working for Xamarin. He spends his days with the awesome documentation team fusing C# and Android into Xamarin documentation with the goal of helping developers create cross-platform mobile applications. His evenings are spent taking his two boys around to their activities and being dragged around by his trusting Samoyed, who never says no to a walk.

William Thomas grew up in Claremont, CA, and developed an interest in computers from a young age. He started out with Flash development, became interested in web design, and then moved on to web development. After attending Cal Poly Pomona to study Computer Science, he began working in 2011, at Flavorus; the Los Angeles-based ticketing company.

Since his graduation, at Cal Poly, William continues to work full time at Flavorus, developing applications for web and mobile devices. He has most recently developed the Flavorus Box Office app for iPhone and iPad using the Xamarin .NET framework.

I'd like to acknowledge my friends and colleagues from Cal Poly Pomona and Flavorus. I truly appreciate the time spent with my professors in the classroom as well as the knowledge and experience I've gained at my workplace.

www.PacktPub.com

Support files, eBooks, discount offers, and more

You might want to visit www.PacktPub.com for support files and downloads related to your book.

Did you know that Packt offers eBook versions of every book published, with PDF and ePub files available? You can upgrade to the eBook version at www.PacktPub.com and as a print book customer, you are entitled to a discount on the eBook copy. Get in touch with us at service@packtpub.com for more details.

At www.PacktPub.com, you can also read a collection of free technical articles, sign up for a range of free newsletters and receive exclusive discounts and offers on Packt books and eBooks.

http://PacktLib.PacktPub.com

Do you need instant solutions to your IT questions? PacktLib is Packt's online digital book library. Here, you can access, read and search across Packt's entire library of books.

Why subscribe?

- Fully searchable across every book published by Packt
- Copy and paste, print and bookmark content
- On demand and accessible via web browser

Free access for Packt account holders

If you have an account with Packt at www.PacktPub.com, you can use this to access PacktLib today and view nine entirely free books. Simply use your login credentials for immediate access.

Table of Contents

Preface

Xamarin has built three core products for developing iOS and Android applications in C#: Xamarin Studio, Xamarin.iOS, and Xamarin.Android. Xamarin gives you direct access to the native APIs on each platform and the flexibility to share C# code among platforms. Using Xamarin and C#, the productivity you get is better than that of Java or Objective-C while maintaining a greater performance output compared to a HTML or JavaScript solution.

In this book, we will develop a real-world sample application to demonstrate what you can do with Xamarin technologies, and build on core platform concepts for iOS and Android. We will also cover advanced topics such as push notifications, retrieving contacts, using a camera, and GPS location. Finally, we will walk through what it takes to submit your application to the Apple App Store and Google Play.

What this book covers

Chapter 1, *Xamarin Setup*, covers the process of installing the appropriate Xamarin software and native SDKs required for performing cross-platform development.

Chapter 2, *Hello Platforms!*, covers creating your first "Hello World" application on iOS and Android, which covers some basic concepts on each platform.

Chapter 3, *Code Sharing Between iOS and Android*, introduces code-sharing techniques and strategies to set up projects that can be used with Xamarin.

Chapter 4, *XamChat – a Cross-platform App*, introduces a sample application that we will be building throughout the book. In this chapter, we will write all the shared code for the application, complete with unit tests.

Chapter 5, *XamChat for iOS*, covers the technique of implementing the iOS user interface for XamChat and various iOS development concepts.

Chapter 6, XamChat for Android, covers the technique of implementing the Android version of XamChat and introduces Android-specific development concepts.

Chapter 7, Deploying and Testing on Devices, explains the painful process of deploying your first application on a device. We also cover why it is important to always test your application on real devices.

Chapter 8, Web Services with Push Notifications, explains the technique of implementing a real backend web service for XamChat using Azure Mobile Services.

Chapter 9, Third-party Libraries, covers the various options to use third-party libraries with Xamarin and how you can even leverage native Java and Objective-C libraries.

Chapter 10, Contacts, Camera, and Location, introduces the library Xamarin.Mobile as a cross-platform library for accessing users' contacts, camera, and GPS location.

Chapter 11, App Store Submission, explains the process of submitting your app to the Apple App Store and Google Play.

What you need for this book

For this book, you will need a Mac computer that at least runs on OS X 10.7 Lion. Apple requires iOS applications to be compiled on a Mac, so our examples throughout the book will use Xamarin Studio on a Mac. You will also need a license of the business edition of Xamarin.Android and Xamarin.iOS. A free 30-day trial is also available. You can try the free Starter edition of Xamarin, but some of the more advanced examples will not work with that edition. Visit `http://xamarin.com/download` to download the appropriate software.

Who this book is for

If you are a developer who is already familiar with C# and you want to start mobile application development with Xamarin, this book is for you. If you have worked with ASP.NET, WPF, WinRT, or Windows Phone, then you will feel right at home using this book to develop native iOS and Android applications.

Conventions

In this book, you will find a number of styles of text that distinguish between different kinds of information. Here are some examples of these styles, and an explanation of their meaning.

Code words in text, database table names, folder names, filenames, file extensions, pathnames, dummy URLs, user input, and Twitter handles are shown as follows: "Create a new folder in the XamChat.Droid project named Core."

A block of code is set as follows:

```
private async void LoadData()
{
  var service = ServiceContainer.Resolve<IWebService>()
    as AzureWebService;

  await service.LoadData();
}
```

Any command-line input or output is written as follows:

```
GoogleAnalytics.Droid: Warning BG8102:
    Class GoogleAnalytics.Tracking.CampaignTrackingService has
    unknown base type android.app.IntentService (BG8102)
    (GoogleAnalytics.Droid)
```

New terms and **important words** are shown in bold. Words that you see on the screen, in menus or dialog boxes for example, appear in the text like this: "To get started, simply right-click on the folder, and select **Get More Components** to launch the store dialog."

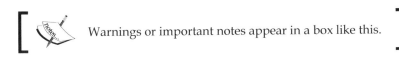

Warnings or important notes appear in a box like this.

Tips and tricks appear like this.

Reader feedback

Feedback from our readers is always welcome. Let us know what you think about this book—what you liked or may have disliked. Reader feedback is important for us to develop titles that you really get the most out of.

To send us general feedback, simply send an e-mail to feedback@packtpub.com, and mention the book title via the subject of your message.

If there is a topic that you have expertise in and you are interested in either writing or contributing to a book, see our author guide on www.packtpub.com/authors.

Customer support

Now that you are the proud owner of a Packt book, we have a number of things to help you to get the most from your purchase.

Downloading the example code

You can download the example code files for all Packt books you have purchased from your account at `http://www.packtpub.com`. If you purchased this book elsewhere, you can visit `http://www.packtpub.com/support` and register to have the files e-mailed directly to you.

Errata

Although we have taken every care to ensure the accuracy of our content, mistakes do happen. If you find a mistake in one of our books—maybe a mistake in the text or the code—we would be grateful if you would report this to us. By doing so, you can save other readers from frustration and help us improve subsequent versions of this book. If you find any errata, please report them by visiting `http://www.packtpub.com/submit-errata`, selecting your book, clicking on the **errata submission form** link, and entering the details of your errata. Once your errata are verified, your submission will be accepted and the errata will be uploaded on our website, or added to any list of existing errata, under the Errata section of that title. Any existing errata can be viewed by selecting your title from `http://www.packtpub.com/support`.

Piracy

Piracy of copyright material on the Internet is an ongoing problem across all media. At Packt, we take the protection of our copyright and licenses very seriously. If you come across any illegal copies of our works, in any form, on the Internet, please provide us with the location address or website name immediately so that we can pursue a remedy.

Please contact us at `copyright@packtpub.com` with a link to the suspected pirated material.

We appreciate your help in protecting our authors, and our ability to bring you valuable content.

Questions

You can contact us at `questions@packtpub.com` if you are having a problem with any aspect of the book, and we will do our best to address it.

1
Xamarin Setup

Xamarin has finally given us the power to develop native iOS, Android, and Mac applications in C#, which is one of our favorite programming languages. There are many advantages of choosing Xamarin to develop mobile applications instead of Java and Objective-C. You can share code between multiple platforms and can be more productive by taking advantage of the advanced language features of C# and the .NET base class libraries. Alternatively, you would have to write the app twice for Android and iOS and lose the benefits of garbage collection in iOS.

In comparison to other techniques of developing cross platform applications with JavaScript and HTML, Xamarin also has some distinct advantages. C# is generally more performant than JavaScript, and Xamarin gives developers direct access to the native APIs on each platform. This allows Xamarin applications to have a native look and perform in a manner similar to their Java or Objective-C counterparts.

Xamarin's tooling works by compiling your C# into a native **ARM** executable that can be packaged as an iOS or Android application. It bundles a stripped-down version of the Mono runtime with your application that only includes the features of the base class libraries your app uses.

In this chapter, we'll set up everything you need to get started on developing with Xamarin. By the end of the chapter, we'll have all the proper SDKs and tools installed and all the developer accounts needed for app store submission.

In this chapter, we will cover:

- An introduction to Xamarin tools and technology
- Installing Xcode, Apple's IDE
- Setting up all Xamarin tools and software
- Setting up the Android emulator
- Enrolling in the iOS Developer Program
- Registering for Google Play

The Xamarin tools

Xamarin has developed three core products for developing cross-platform applications: **Xamarin Studio** (formerly MonoDevelop), **Xamarin.iOS** (formerly MonoTouch), and **Xamarin.Android** (formerly Mono for Android). These tools allow developers to leverage the native libraries on iOS and Android and are built on the Mono runtime.

Mono, an open source implementation of C# and the .NET framework, was originally developed by Novell to be used on Linux operating systems. Since iOS and Android are similarly based on Linux, Novell was able to develop MonoTouch and Mono for Android as products to target the new mobile platforms. Shortly after their release, another company acquired Novell, and let the Mono team go. Very shortly after, Xamarin was founded to focus completely on these tools for developing with C# on iOS and Android.

Getting a development machine ready for developing cross-platform application development can take some time. And to make matters worse, Apple and Google both have their own requirements for development on their respective platforms. Let's go over what needs to be installed on your machine.

To get started on iOS, we'll need to install the following:

- **Xcode**: Apple's core IDE for developing iOS and Mac applications in Objective-C
- **Xcode Command Line Tools**: These are installed inside Xcode, and provide common Command Line Tools and scripting languages that developers would find useful, such as Subversion or SVN, Git, Perl, Ruby.
- **The Mono runtime for Mac**: This is required for compiling and running C# programs on OS X
- **Xamarin.iOS**: This is Xamarin's core product for iOS development

Android also requires the following software to be installed to get started:

- **Java**: This is the core runtime for running Java applications on OS X
- **Android SDK**: This contains Google's standard SDK, device drivers, and emulators for native Android development
- **The Mono runtime for Mac**: This is required for compiling and running C# programs on OS X
- **Xamarin.Android**: This is Xamarin's core product for Android development

Each of these will take some time to download and install. If you can access a fast internet connection, it will help speed up the installation and set up process. With everything ready to go, let's move ahead step by step, and hopefully, we can skip a few dead ends you might otherwise run into.

It is important to note that Xamarin can also be used on Windows and Visual Studio, even though it is not covered in this book. A Mac is required for iOS development, so Windows developers must connect Visual Studio to a Mac to compile for iOS. Luckily, most of what we learn in this book can be directly applied to using Xamarin on Windows.

Installing Xcode

To make things progress more smoothly, let's start off by installing Xcode for Mac. Along with Apple's IDE, it will also install the most commonly used developer tools on the Mac. Make sure you have at least OS X 10.8 (Mountain Lion), and locate Xcode in the App Store as shown in the following screenshot:

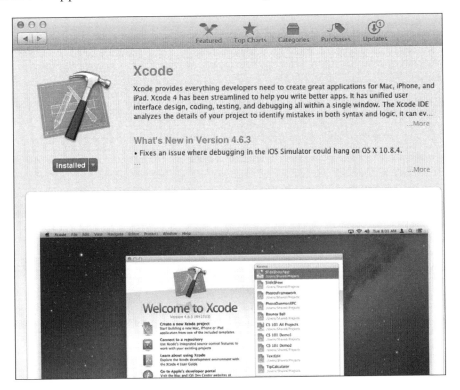

This will take quite some time to download and install. I'd recommend taking the time to enjoy a nice cup of coffee or work on another project at the same time.

When that is out of the way, launch Xcode for the first time and progress through the initial startup dialog. Next, navigate to **Xcode | Preferences...** to open Xcode's main settings dialog.

In the **Downloads | Components** tab, you'll notice several additional packages you can install inside Xcode. Go ahead and install the Command Line Tools. Optionally, you can install older iOS simulators, but we can just use the default one for the content in this book. When you're finished, your Xcode's **Components** section should look something similar to the following screenshot:

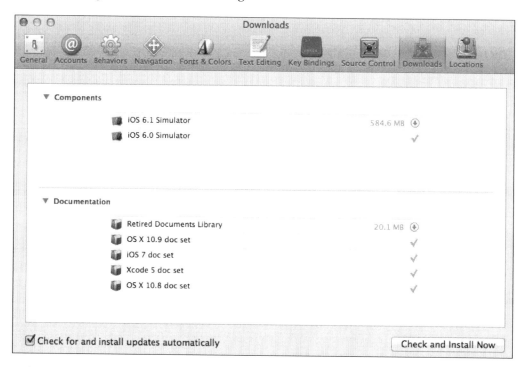

Installing Xcode installs the iOS SDK, which is a requirement for iOS development in general. As a restriction from Apple, the iOS SDK can only run on a Mac. Xamarin has done everything possible to make sure they follow Apple's guidelines for iOS, such as dynamic code generation. Xamarin's tools also leverage features of Xcode wherever possible to avoid reinventing the wheel.

Installing Xamarin

After installing Xcode, there are several other dependencies that need to be installed in order to start developing with Xamarin's tools. Luckily, Xamarin has improved the experience by creating a neat all-in-one installer.

Install the free Xamarin Starter Edition with the following steps:

1. Go to http://Xamarin.com and click on the large **Download Now** button.

2. Fill out some basic information about yourself.

3. Download `XamarinInstaller.dmg` and mount the disk image.

4. Launch `Install Xamarin.app` and accept any OS X security warnings that appear.

5. Progress through the installer, the default options will work fine. You can optionally install Xamarin.Mac, but that topic is not covered in this book.

The Xamarin installer will download and install prerequisites such as the Mono runtime, Java, the Android SDK (including the Android emulator and tools), and everything else you need to be up and running.

You will end up with something similar to what is shown in the following screenshot, and we can move on to conquer bigger topics in cross platform development:

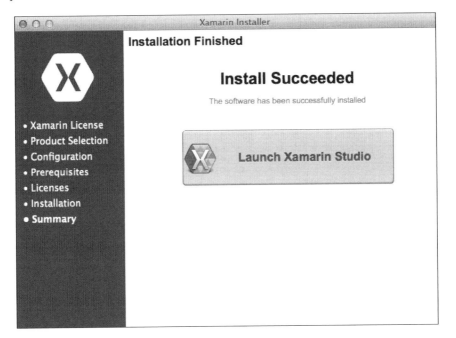

Xamarin has several editions, so it is good know the differences to determine which license you may need to purchase. The editions are as follows:

- **Starter Edition**: This is available to individuals only, and it has a limit of 64 KB of compiled user code

- **Indie Edition**: This is available to individuals only, and it does not include Visual Studio support

- **Business Edition**: This is available for companies; it adds features for Visual Studio and includes better Xamarin product support

- **Enterprise Edition**: This includes prime components in the Xamarin Component Store for free and much more Xamarin product support such as hotfixes and less than 24 hours response time to issues

Setting up the Android emulator

The Android emulator has historically been known to be sluggish compared to developing on a physical device. To help solve this issue, Google has produced a new x86 emulator that supports hardware acceleration on desktop computers. It isn't installed by default in the **Android Virtual Device (AVD)** Manager, so let's set that up.

The x86 Android Emulator can be installed by performing the following steps:

1. Open Xamarin Studio.

2. Launch **Tools | Open Android SDK Manager...**.

3. Scroll down to **Extras**; install **Intel x86 Emulator Accelerator (HAXM)**.

4. Scroll to **Android 4.2.2 (API 17)**; install **Intel x86 Atom System Image**.

5. Optionally, install any other packages you are interested in. At a minimum, make sure you have everything that the Android SDK Manager selects for you to install by default.

6. Close the **Android SDK Manager** and switch back to Xamarin Studio.

7. Launch **Tools | Open AVD Manager...**.

8. Click on **New...**.

9. Enter an AVD name of your choice, such as x86 Emulator.

10. Pick a generic device that will be appropriately sized for your display, such as the **4.0 inch WVGA**.

11. As **Target**, make sure you select **Intel x86 Atom System Image**.

12. After creating the device, go ahead and click on **Start...** to make sure the emulator runs properly.

The emulator will take some time to start up, so it is a good idea to leave the emulator running while performing Android development. Xamarin is using the standard Android tools here, so you would have the same issue while performing Android development with Java. If everything starts properly, you will see an Android boot screen followed by a virtual Android device ready for deploying applications from Xamarin Studio as shown in the following screenshot:

Enrolling in the iOS Developer Program

To deploy to an iOS device, Apple requires a membership to its iOS Developer Program. Membership is $99 USD per year and gives you access to deploy 200 devices for development purposes. You also get access to test servers for implementing more advanced iOS features such as in-app purchases, push notifications, and iOS Game Center. Testing your Xamarin.iOS applications on a physical device is important, so I recommend getting an account prior to starting iOS development. Performance is very different in a simulator running on your desktop versus a real mobile device. There are also a few Xamarin-specific optimizations that only occur when running on the device. We'll fully cover the reasons for testing your apps on devices in later chapters.

Signing up for the iOS Developer Program can be performed through the following steps:

1. Go to `https://developer.apple.com/programs/ios`.

2. Click on **Enroll Now**.

3. Sign in with an existing iTunes account or create a new one. This can't be changed later, so choose the one that is appropriate for your company.

4. Enroll either as an individual or a company. Both are priced at $99; but, registering as a company will require paperwork to be faxed to Apple with the assistance of your company's accountant.

5. Review the developer agreement.

6. Fill out Apple's survey for developers.

7. Purchase the $99 developer registration.

8. Wait for a confirmation e-mail.

You should receive an email that looks something like the following screenshot within two business days:

From here, we can continue setting up your account.

1. Either click on **Login** from the e-mail you received or go to `https://itunesconnect.apple.com`.

2. Log in with your earlier iTunes account.

3. Agree to any additional agreements that appear on the home page of your dashboard.

4. From the iTunes Connect dashboard, go to **Contracts, Tax, and Banking**.

5. In this section, you will see three columns for **Contact Info**, **Bank Info**, and **Tax Info**.

6. Fill out the appropriate information for your account in all of these sections. Assistance from an accountant will most likely be needed for a company account.

When all is said and done, your **Contracts, Tax, and Banking** section should look something like the following screenshot:

With your iOS Developer account successfully registered, you will now be able to deploy to iOS devices and publish your apps to the Apple App Store.

Registering as a Google Play developer

Unlike iOS, deploying your applications to Android devices is free and just requires a few changes in your device settings. A Google Play developer account has only a one-time fee of $25 and doesn't have to be renewed each year. However, just like iOS, you will need a Google Play account to develop in-app purchases, push notifications, or Google Play Game Services. I would recommend setting up an account ahead of time if you inevitably plan on submitting an app to Google Play or need to implement one of these features.

To register as a developer for Google Play, perform the following steps:

1. Go to `https://play.google.com/apps/publish`.

2. Log in with an existing Google Account, or create a new one. This can't be changed later, so choose the one that is appropriate for your company if needed.

3. Accept the agreement and enter your credit card information.

4. Choose a developer name and enter other important information for your account. Again, choose names appropriate for your company to be seen by users in the app store.

If you get everything filled out correctly, you will end up with the following Google Play Developer Console:

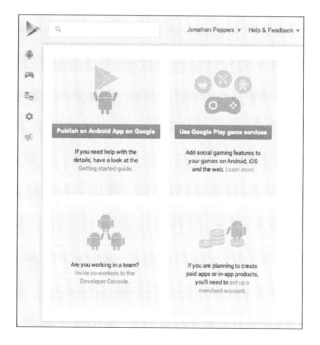

If you plan on selling paid apps or in-app purchases, at this point, I would recommend setting up your **Google Merchant Account**. This will enable Google to pay you the proceeds toward your app sales by applying the appropriate tax laws in your country. If setting this up for your company, I would recommend getting the assistance of your company's accountant or bookkeeper.

The following are the steps to set up a Google Merchant Account:

1. Click on the **set up a merchant account** button.

2. Log in with your Google account a second time.

3. Fill out the appropriate information for selling apps: address, phone number, tax information, and a display name to appear on your customers' credit card bill.

When done, you will notice that the help tip for setting up a merchant account is now missing from the developer console, as shown in the following screenshot:

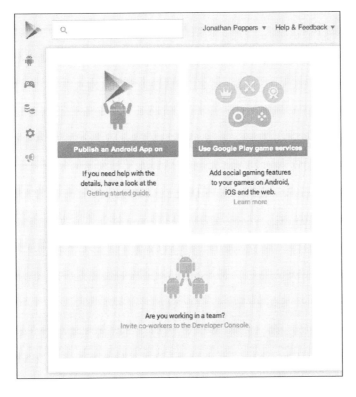

At this point, one would think our account would be fully set up, but there is one more crucial step prior to being able to sell apps: we have to enter the banking information.

Setting up banking for your Google Merchant Account can be performed with the following steps:

1. Go back to the Google Play **Developer Console** at `https://play.google.com/apps/publish`.

2. Click on the **Financial Reports** section.

3. Click on the small link titled **Visit your merchant account for details**.

4. You should see a warning indicating that you do not have a bank account set up. Click on the **Specify a Bank Account** link to get started.

5. Enter your banking information. Again, a company accountant might be needed.

6. In a few days, look for a small deposit in your account from Google.

7. Confirm the amount by going to `http://checkout.google.com/sell`.

8. Click on the **Settings** tab, then **Financials**.

9. Next, click on **Verify Account**.

10. Enter the amount that appeared on your bank account and click on **Verify deposit**.

Your Google Merchant Account is also the place where you can cancel or refund customer orders. Google Play is different from the iOS App Store, in that all customer issues are directed to the developers.

Summary

In this chapter, we discussed Xamarin's core products for developing Android and iOS applications in C#: Xamarin Studio, Xamarin.iOS, and Xamarin.Android. We installed Xcode and then ran the Xamarin all-in-one installer, which installs Java, the Android SDK, Xamarin Studio, Xamarin.iOS, and Xamarin.Android. We set up the x86 Android Emulator for a faster, more fluid experience when debugging applications. Finally we set up iOS and Google Play developer accounts for distributing our applications.

In this chapter, you should have acquired everything you need to get started on building cross-platform applications with Xamarin. Your development computer should be ready to go and you should have all the native SDKs installed and ready for creating the next great app to take the world by storm.

The concepts in this chapter will set us up for more advanced topics that will require the proper software installed as well as developer accounts with Apple and Google. We will be deploying applications to real devices and implementing more advanced features such as push notifications. In the next chapter, we'll create our first iOS and Android application and cover the basics of each platform.

2
Hello Platforms!

If you are familiar with developing applications using Visual Studio on Windows, then using Xamarin Studio should be very straightforward. Xamarin uses the same concept of a **solution** that contains one or more **projects**, and there are now several new project types for iOS and Android applications. There are also several project templates to jumpstart your development of common applications.

Xamarin Studio supports several out of the box project types including standard .NET class libraries and console applications. You cannot natively develop Windows applications on a Mac with Xamarin Studio, but you can certainly develop the shared code portion of your application in Xamarin Studio. We'll elaborate on sharing code in the later chapters, but keep in mind that Xamarin enables you to share a common C# backend between nearly any platforms that support C#.

In this chapter, we will cover:

- Hello World for iOS
- Apple's MVC pattern
- Xcode and storyboards
- Hello World for Android
- Android activities
- Xamarin's Android designer

Building your first iOS application

Launch Xamarin Studio and start a new solution. Just like in Visual Studio, there are lots of project types that can be created from the **New Solution** dialog. Xamarin Studio, formerly **MonoDevelop**, supports the development of many different types of projects such as C# console applications targeting the Mono runtime, NUnit test projects, and even other languages besides C#, such as VB or C++.

Xamarin Studio supports the following project types for iOS:

- **iPhone or iPad project**: This is the default project targeting an iPhone or iPad using XIB files for user interface layout. This is an older format that is fine to use, but doesn't have as many options as storyboards.

- **iPhone or iPad storyboard project**: This is a project that uses storyboards for laying out the UI. Storyboards were released with iOS 5 and are the more modern ways of modifying UI layouts.

- **Universal project**: This is a project that can support either XIB or storyboards. Supports both iPad and iPhone in the same application.

- **iOS binding project**: This is an iOS project that can create C# bindings for an Objective-C library.

- **iOS unit test project**: This is a special iOS application project that can run NUnit tests.

- **iOS library project**: This is a class library used within other iOS application projects.

To get started, navigate to **iOS | iPhone Storyboard** and, create a **Single View Application** in the directory of your choice, as seen in the following screenshot.

You'll notice that several files and folders are automatically created from the project template. These files are as follows:

- `Resources`: This directory will contain any images or plain files that you want to be copied directly to your application bundle.

- `AppDelegate.cs`: This is Apple's main class that handles application-level events in your app.

- `*ViewController.cs`: This is the controller that represents the first screen in your app. It will have the same name as your project.

- `Info.plist`: This is Apple's version of a **manifest** file that can declare various settings for your application.

- `Main.cs`: This file contains the standard entry point for a C# program: `static void Main()`. It's most likely that you will not need to modify this file.

- `MainStoryboard.storyboard`: This is the storyboard definition file for your application. It will contain the layouts for the views in your app, list of controllers, and the transitions for navigating throughout your app.

Now, let's run the application to see what we get by default from the project template. Click on the large play button in the top-left corner of Xamarin Studio. You will be greeted by the simulator running your first iOS application as seen in the following screenshot:

So far, your app is just a plain white screen, which is not very exciting; but, let's get a little more background on iOS development before moving forward.

Depending on your application's minimum iOS target, you can also run the application on an iOS 6 or iOS 7 simulator. Apple also provides simulators for iPad and different devices such as the iPad, iPhone 4, and iPhone 5. It is also important to know that these are simulators and not emulators. An emulator will run an encapsulated version of the mobile OS (just as Android does). Emulators generally exhibit slower performance but give you a closer replica of the real OS. Apple's simulators run in native Mac applications and are not true operating systems. The benefit is that they are very fast in comparison to Android emulators.

Understanding Apple's MVC pattern

Before getting too far with iOS development, it is really important to get a foundation with Apple's design pattern for developing on iOS. You may have used the **MVC (Model View Controller)** pattern with other technologies such as **ASP. NET**, but Apple implements this paradigm in a slightly different way.

The **MVC** design pattern includes the following:

- **Model**: This is the backend business logic that drives the application. This can be any code that, for example, makes web requests to a server or saves data to a local **SQLite** database.

- **View**: This is the actual user interface seen on the screen. In iOS terms, this is any class that derives from UIView. Examples are toolbars, buttons, and anything else the user would see on the screen and interact with.

- **Controller**: This is the workhorse of the MVC pattern. The controller interacts with the model layer and updates the view layer with the results. Just like the view layer, any controller class would derive from UIViewController. This is where a good portion of the code in iOS applications resides.

The following image shows the MVC design pattern:

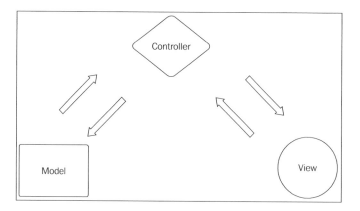

To understand this pattern better, let's walk through the following example of a common scenario:

1. We have an iOS application with a search box that needs to query a website for a list of jobs.

2. The user will enter some text into the `UITextField` textbox and click on the `UIButton` button to start the search. This is the view layer.

3. Some code will respond to the button by interacting with the view, display a `UIActivityIndicatorView` spinner, and call a method in another class to perform the search. This is the controller layer.

4. A web request will be made in the called class and a list of jobs will be returned asynchronously. This is the model layer.

5. The controller will then update the view with the list of jobs and hide the spinner.

> For more information on Apple's MVC pattern, see the documentation at `https://developer.apple.com/library/mac/documentation/general/conceptual/devpedia-cocoacore/MVC.html`.

A point to note is that you are free to do anything you want in the model layer of your application. This is where we can use plain C# classes that can be reused on other platforms such as Android. This includes any functionality using the C# **Base Class Libraries (BCL)**, such as working with web services or a database. We'll dive deeper into cross-platform architecture and code-sharing concepts later in the book.

Using Xcode and storyboards

Since our plain white application is quite boring, let's modify the view layer of our application with some controls. To do this, we will modify the `MainStoryboard.storyboard` file in your project in Xcode. At the time of writing this book, Xamarin Studio will launch and communicate with Xcode to modify iOS layout files. An iOS design tool in Xamarin Studio is currently in development and will function very similarly to Xcode.

Let's add some controls to our app by performing the following steps:

1. Open the project you created earlier in this chapter in Xamarin Studio.

2. Double-click on the `MainStoryboard.storyboard` file.

3. Xcode will launch and you will see the layout for the single controller in your application.

4. In the tree structure on the left, you'll see that your controller contains a single view in its layout hierarchy.

5. In the bottom-right corner, you'll notice a toolbox containing several types of objects that you can drag-and-drop onto the view associated with the controller.

6. In the search box, search for `UILabel` and drag the label onto the view at a location of your choice.

7. Click on the label to select it and then click on it again to edit the text of the label to anything you wish.

8. Likewise, search for `UIButton` and drag the button onto the view somewhere above or below the label. You may edit the text on the button in the same way as you did on the label, if you wish.

9. Save the storyboard file by pressing *command* + *S*.

10. Switch back to Xamarin Studio and run the application.

Your application should start looking a lot more like a real app as seen in the following screenshot:

Now you might be wondering about adding user interaction options to the app at this point. In Xcode, we can make an **outlet** that will make each view visible from C#. An outlet is a reference to a view in a storyboard or XIB file that will be filled out with an instance of the view at runtime. You can compare this concept to naming a control in other technologies such as ASP.NET, WebForms, or **WPF (Windows Presentation Foundation)**. A Xamarin Studio behind-the-scenes tool will create a property in a **partial class**, which gives you access to the label and button from your controller. Additionally, you can wire an **action** from a storyboard or XIB file, which is a method that will be called when an event occurs. Xamarin Studio exposes Xcode actions as partial methods to be implemented in your classes. It is generally cleaner from a C# developer's perspective to just use the C# event, but it is neat to have both options.

Let's add some interactions to the app as follows:

1. Switch back to Xamarin Studio.
2. Double-click on the `MainStoryboard.storyboard` file again.
3. In the top-right corner, you'll notice a toggle menu labeled **Editor**; click on the button that looks like a tuxedo.
4. A split view will appear with your layout on the left and an `Objective-C` header file on the right. In future, you can click on the button to the left of the tuxedo to go back to the other view.
5. Right-click and hold on the label and drag it to the header file below the `@interace` declaration and release it. A blue line attached to your mouse pointer appears as you do this and an indicator will appear in the header file to tell you when you can release it.
6. In the outlet popup, you can see the **Name** field. Pick a name for the label's outlet, for example, `label`.
7. Click on **Connect**, you will see `IBOutlet UILabel *label;` appear in the header file.
8. Repeat this process for the button, selecting a name such as `button`.
9. Save the header and storyboard files by pressing *command* + *S*.
10. Switch back to Xamarin Studio and run the application.

If you get lost in Xcode, don't fret. It is a very different experience compared to Visual Studio if you are used to Microsoft tools. Apple is big on minimalistic interfaces, so it can be difficult to pick up their workflow without a detailed explanation. Coming from a WPF and WinForms background, I initially had trouble figuring out how to use Xcode's interface myself.

Here is what the first outlet dialog should look like:

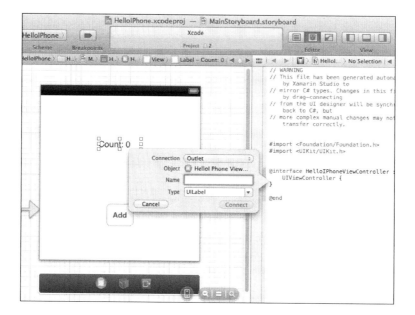

Now that we have two outlets defined, two new properties will be available from your controller. Expand the *ViewController.cs file in your solution and open the *ViewController.designer.cs file. You will see your properties defined as follows:

```
[Outlet]
MonoTouch.UIKit.UILabel label { get; set; }

[Outlet]
MonoTouch.UIKit.UIButton button { get; set; }
```

It is not a good idea to modify this file since Xamarin Studio may rebuild it if you make further changes in Xcode. Nevertheless, it is good practice to learn how things actually work behind the scenes.

Open your *ViewController.cs file and let's enter the following code in your controller's ViewDidLoad method:

```
public override void ViewDidLoad()
{
  base.ViewDidLoad();

  int count = 0;
  button.TouchUpInside += (sender, e) =>
  label.Text = string.Format("Count: {0}", ++count);
}
```

When ViewDidLoad is called for the first time, your controller's view is loaded. This happens once in the lifetime of your controller. We subscribed to the TouchUpInside event, which is fired when the button is clicked; iOS does not have a click event that is commonly used on Windows platforms. We also used C#'s convenient lambda expression syntax to update the label when the event is fired.

Run your application and you will be able to interact with your button and increment the value displayed in the label, as shown in the following screenshot:

Next, we need to make a transition from one controller to another. To do this, iOS has a concept called **segue**, which is basically some kind of animation that switches from one controller to the next. There are several types of segues, but the most common segue slides a new controller from the left or bottom of the screen.

Now let's add a second controller to the application as follows:

1. Return to your project in Xamarin Studio.

2. Double-click on the `MainStoryboard.storyboard` file.

3. Drag a new controller from the object library in the bottom-left corner next to the first controller.

4. Click on the controller to select it.

5. In the property pane on the top-right corner, click on the identity inspector tab (third tab from the left).

6. Under the **Custom Class** section, enter a name such as `SecondController` for the controller into the **Class** field.

7. Now let's add a segue for transition from the first controller to this one. Right-click and hold on the button from the original controller to your new controller. A blue line will appear followed by a small pop-up menu.

8. Select **modal** from the pop-up menu.

9. Save the storyboard files by pressing *command + S*.

10. Switch back to Xamarin Studio and run the application.

Since we've set up a modal segue from the first controller's button, your second controller will appear while clicking it. However, there isn't a way to exit the new controller yet. If you return to Xamarin Studio, you'll notice that a `SecondController.cs` file and `SecondController.designer.cs` file have automatically been created for you.

Let's add a button to your second controller as follows:

1. Return to Xamarin Studio.

2. Double-click on the `MainStoryboard.storyboard` file.

3. Drag a button from the object library onto the second controller.

4. Set the title of the button to `Close`.

5. Under the **Editor** menu, click on the button that looks like a tuxedo.

6. Right-click and hold on the button and drag it to your header file to create a new outlet and name it `Close`.

7. Save the header and storyboard file by pressing *command + S*.

8. Switch back to Xamarin Studio.

9. Open the `SecondController.cs` file and add the following method:

```
public override void ViewDidLoad()
{
  base.ViewDidLoad();
  close.TouchUpInside +=(sender, e) => DismissViewController(true,
null);
}
```

If you compile and run your application, clicking on the button will increment the value on the label and display the modal second controller. You can then close the second controller by tapping on **Close**. Notice the neat sliding animation; iOS automatically applies these kinds of transition effects, which are very easy to customize on iOS.

Since we have gone over the basics of laying out controls in Xcode and interacting with outlets in C#, let's go over the standard lifecycle of an iOS application. The primary location for handling application-level events is in the `AppDelegate` class.

If you open your `AppDelegate.cs` file, you can override the following methods:

- `FinishedLaunching`: This is the first entry point for the application, which should return `true`.

- `DidEnterBackground`: This means the user clicked on the home button on their device or another instance, such as a phone call, came to the foreground. You should perform any action needed to save the user's progress or state of the UI as the iOS may kill your application once pushed to the background. While your application is in the background, the user could be navigating through the home screen or opening other apps. Your application is effectively paused in memory until resumed by the user.

- `WillEnterForeground`: This means the user has reopened your application from the background. You might need to perform other actions here such as refreshing the data on the screen and so on.

- `OnResignActivation`: This happens if the operating system displays a system pop up on top of your application. Examples of this are calendar reminders or the menu the user can swipe down from the top of the screen.

- `OnActivated`: This happens immediately after the `OnResignActivation` method is executed as the user returns to your app.

- `ReceiveMemoryWarning`: This is a warning from the operating system to free up the memory in your application. It is not commonly required with Xamarin because of C#'s garbage collector, but if there are any heavy objects such as images throughout your app, this is a good place to dispose them. If enough memory cannot be freed, the operating system could terminate your application.

- `HandleOpenUrl`: This is called if you implement a **URL scheme**, which is the iOS equivalent of file extension associations on a desktop platform. If you register your app to open different types of files or URLs, this method will be called.

Likewise, in your `*ViewController.cs` file, you can override the following methods on your controller:

- `ViewDidLoad`: This occurs when the view associated with your controller is loaded. It will occur only once on devices running iOS 6 or higher.

- `ViewWillAppear`: This occurs prior to your view appearing on the screen. If there are any views that need to be refreshed while navigating throughout your app, this is generally the best place to do it.

- `ViewDidAppear`: This occurs after the completion of any transition animations and your view is displayed on the screen. In some uncommon situations, you might need to perform actions here instead of in `ViewWillAppear`.

- `ViewWillDisappear`: This method is called prior to your view being hidden. You might need to perform some clean-up operations here.

- `ViewDidDisappear`: This occurs after any transition animations are completed for displaying a different controller on the screen. Just like the methods for appearing, this occurs after `ViewWillDisappear`.

Apart from these methods, there are other methods but many are deprecated for iOS 6 and above. Familiarize yourself with Apple's documentation at `http://developer.apple.com/library/ios`. It is very helpful to read the documentation on each class and method when trying to understand how Apple's APIs work. Learning how to read (not necessarily code) Objective-C is also a useful skill to learn so that you are able to convert Objective-C examples to C# when developing iOS applications.

Building your first Android application

Setting up an Android application in Xamarin Studio is just as easy as it is for iOS. It's also very similar to the experiences in Visual Studio. Xamarin Studio includes several project templates that are specific for Android to jump-start your development.

Xamarin Studio includes the following project templates:

- **Android application**: A standard Android application that targets the newest Android SDKs installed on your machine
- **Android Honeycomb application**: A project that targets Android Honeycomb, which is **API (Application Programming Interface)** level 12 and above
- **Android Ice Cream Sandwich application**: A project that targets Android Ice Cream Sandwich, which is API level 15 and above
- **Android library project**: A class library that can only be referenced by Android application projects
- **Android Java bindings library**: A project for setting up a Java library to be called from C#
- **Android OpenGL application**: A project template to use low-level OpenGL for 3D or 2D rendering
- **Android unit test project**: A project for running NUnit tests on Android

Launch Xamarin Studio and start a new solution. From the **New Solution** dialog, create a new **Android Application** under the **Android** section.

You will end up with a solution that looks something like the following screenshot:

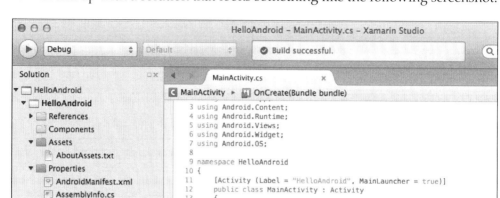

You'll notice that the following files and folders specific to Android have been created for you:

- The `Assets` folder: This directory will contain files with a `build` action of `AndroidAsset`. This folder will contain raw files to be bundled with an Android application.

- `Properties/AndroidManifest.xml`: This file contains standard declarations about your Android applications, such as the application name, ID, and permissions.

- The `Resources` folder: Resources are images, layouts, strings, and so on that can be loaded via Android's resource system. Each file will have an ID generated in `Resources.designer.cs` that you can use to load the resource.

- The `Resources/drawable` folder: Any images used by your application are generally placed here.

- The `Resources/layout` folder: This contains any `*.axml` (Android XML) files that Android uses to declare UIs. Layouts can be used for an entire **activity**, **fragment**, **dialog**, or **child control** to be displayed on the screen.

- The `Resources/values` folder: This contains XML files to declare key-value pairs for strings (and other types) throughout an application. This is how localization for multiple languages is normally set up on Android.

- `MainActivity.cs`: This is the `MainLauncher` action and the first activity of your Android application. There is no `static void Main` function in Android apps; execution begins on the activity that has `MainLauncher` set to `true`.

Now let's perform the following steps to run the application:

1. Click on the play button to compile and run the application.

2. A **Select Device** dialog will appear.

3. Select the emulator of your choice and click on **Start Emulator**. If you have set up the x86 emulator in *Chapter 1, Xamarin Setup,* I would recommend using it.

4. Wait a few seconds for the emulator to start. Once it starts, it is a good idea to leave it running as long as you are performing Android development.

5. You should see the emulator now enabled in the list of devices; select it, and click on **OK**.

6. The very first time you deploy to an emulator or device, Xamarin Studio will have to install a few things such as the Mono shared runtime and Android platform tools.

7. Switch over to the Android emulator.

8. Your application will appear.

When all is done, you have deployed your first Android application, complete with a single button. Your app will look like the following screenshot:

Android activities

The Android operating system is very focused on the concept of an activity. An activity is a task or unit of work that users can perform on their screen. For example, users would perform a **phone activity** to dial a number and carry out a second activity to interact with their address book to locate the number. Each Android application is a collection of one or more activities that users can launch and press the hardware's back key on their device to exit or cancel. The users' history is kept in the Android **back stack**, which you can manipulate from code in special cases. When a new activity starts, the previous one is paused and maintained in memory for later use, unless the operating system is running low on memory.

Activities are loosely coupled with each other; in some ways, you can think of them as having completely separate states from one another in memory. Static classes, properties, and fields will persist the life of the application, but the common practice is to pass a state in an Android **bundle**. This is useful when passing an identifier for an item displayed in a list to edit that item in a new activity.

Activities have the following lifecycle callback methods that you can override:

- `OnCreate`: This is the first method called when your activity is created. Set up your views and perform other loading logic here. Most importantly, you will call `SetContentView` here to set up your activity's view.

- `OnResume`: This is called when your activity's view is visible on the screen. It is called if your activity is displayed for the first time and when the user returns to it from another activity.

- `OnPause`: This is called to notify that the user has left your activity. It can happen prior to navigating to a new activity within your app, locking the screen, or hitting the home button. Assume that the user may not return, so you need to save any changes the user made here.

- `OnStart`: This occurs immediately before `OnResume` when the activity's view is about to be displayed on the screen. It occurs when an activity starts and when a user returns to it from another activity.

- `OnStop`: This occurs immediately after `OnPause` when the activity's view is no longer displayed on the screen.

- `OnRestart`: This method occurs when the user returns to your activity from a previous activity.

- `OnActivityResult`: This method is used to communicate with other activities in other applications on Android. It is used in conjunction with `StartActivityForResult`; for example, you would use this to interact with the Facebook application to login a user.

- **OnDestroy**: This is called when your activity is about to be freed from memory. Perform any additional clean-up that could help the operating system here, such as disposing any other heavyweight objects the activity was using.

A flowchart of the Android lifecycle is as follows:

Unlike iOS, Android does not enforce any design patterns upon its developers. However, it is not possible to get away without understanding the Android activity lifecycle to some degree. Many concepts with activities are parallel to controllers on iOS, for example, OnStart is equivalent to ViewWillAppear and OnResume is equivalent to ViewDidAppear.

Other methods to note when working with activities are as follows:

- **StartActivity(Type type)**: This method starts a new activity within your application and passes no extra information to the activity.

- `StartActivity(Intent intent)`: This is an overload method to start a new activity with `Intent`. This gives you the ability to pass additional information to the new activity, and you can also launch activities in other applications.

- `StartActivityForResult`: This method starts a new activity with the anticipation of receiving `OnActivityResult` when the activity's operation is completed.

- `Finish`: This will close the current activity and invoke `OnDestroy` when it is completely closed and no longer displayed on the screen. Depending on what is currently on the back stack, the user will return to a previous activity or the home screen.

- `SetContentView`: This method sets the primary view to be displayed for an activity. It should be called within the `OnCreate` method prior to the activity being displayed on the screen.

- `FindViewById`: This is a method to locate the view displayed in your activity. It has a generic version to return a view of the appropriate type.

You can think of `intent` as an object that describes the transition from one activity to another. You can pass additional data through intents as well as modify how the activity is displayed and modify the user's navigation history.

In addition to activities, Android has the concept of a fragment. You can think of a fragment to be a miniature activity that is displayed inside a parent activity. Fragments are useful for reusing different pieces of a UI throughout your apps and can also help you implement split screen navigation on tablets.

Xamarin's Android designer

The default template for Android projects has a little more built-in functionality than iOS. Android user interface layouts are defined in XML files that are readable by humans and editable. However, Xamarin Studio has provided an excellent design tool that allows you to drag-and-drop controls to define your Android layouts. Let's add some more features to your application and start using the Android designer.

Return to Xamarin Studio and carry out the following steps to add features to your app:

1. Open the Android project you created earlier in this chapter in Xamarin Studio.
2. Under **Resources | layout** in your project, open `Main.axml`.
3. You will see the Android designer open in Xamarin Studio.

4. Drag **TextView** from the **Toolbox** section on the right to the layout just above the button labeled **Hello World, Click Me!**.

5. Type some default text such as Count: 0 into the label.

6. In the **Properties** pane on the right, you'll see the **id** value is set to @+id/ textView1. Let's change it to @+id/myText to be consistent with the button.

7. While we're here, go ahead and change the text on the button to something more appropriate such as Add.

8. Click on the play button to compile and run the application. If you still have the Android emulator, you can simply switch to it. Otherwise, you will have to start it again.

Your Android application will now look identical to the changes you made in the designer, as follows:

Now, let's interact with the new label from the code. Switch back to Xamarin Studio and open MainActivity.cs. Let's modify the activity to interact with the **TextView** field instead of the button. We use the FindViewById method to retrieve a view by the ID we set up in the layout file. Xamarin Studio has also autogenerated a static class named Resource for referencing your identifiers.

So let's retrieve the instance of the **TextView** field by placing this code in OnCreate as follows:

```
TextView text = FindViewById<TextView>(Resource.Id.myText);
```

The Resource class is a static class that the Xamarin designer will populate for you. For future reference, you may have to build your Android project for new IDs and other resources to show up in your C# files in Xamarin Studio.

Next, let's update the Click event on the button:

```
button.Click += delegate
{
  text.Text = string.Format("Count: ", ++count);
};
```

This will rewire the button to update the text in **TextView** instead of on the button itself. Now if we run the application, we'll get an Android app that functions identically to the iOS one in the previous chapter. The Android app will look like the following screenshot:

Since we've added some of our own views to our layout, let's add a second activity to build on our understanding of activities in Android.

Return to Xamarin Studio and perform the following steps:

1. If necessary, open the Android project you created earlier in the chapter in Xamarin Studio.

2. Create a new Android activity in the project under the **Android** section. Name it SecondActivity.cs.

3. Under **Resources** | **layouts**, create a new Android layout named Second.axml.

4. Open SecondActivity.cs and, add the following code to OnCreate:

   ```
   SetContentView(Resource.Layouts.Second);
   ```

5. Open SecondActivity.cs, add the following line of code to the Click event of your button:

   ```
   StartActivity(typeof(SecondActivity));
   ```

6. Open Second.axml and drag a button into the view. Set its text to Finish, for example, and set its ID to @+id/finish.

7. Finally, open SecondActivity.cs and add the following lines to its OnCreate method:

   ```
   var finish = FindViewById<Button>(Resource.Id.finish);
   finish.Click += (sender, e) => Finish();
   ```

8. Build and run your application.

Your application's button will now launch a new activity in addition to incrementing the count on the label. Once SecondActivity is visible, you can click on its button to finish the activity and return to the first activity. Down the road, if you need to pass information from one activity to another, you will need to create an Intent object to pass to StartActivity. The second activity in your app is shown in the following screenshot:

Summary

In this chapter, we created our first iOS application in Xamarin Studio. We covered Apple's MVC design pattern to better understand the relationship between UIViewController and UIView. We also covered how to use Xcode's design tool and how it integrates with Xamarin Studio. Next, we created our first Android application in Xamarin Studio and learned about the activity lifecycle in Android. We also used Xamarin's Android designer to make changes to Android layouts.

From the topics covered in this chapter, you should be fairly confident when developing simple apps for iOS and Android using Xamarin's tools. You should have a basic understanding of the native SDKs and design patterns to accomplish tasks on iOS and Android.

In the next chapter, we'll cover various techniques to share code across platforms with Xamarin Studio. We'll go over different ways to architect your cross-platform applications and how to set up Xamarin Studio projects and solutions.

3
Code Sharing Between iOS and Android

Xamarin Studio tools promise to share a good portion of your code between iOS and Android while taking advantage of the native APIs on each platform where possible. This is the equivalent of an exercise in software engineering more than a programming skill or having the knowledge of each platform. To architect a Xamarin Studio application to enable code sharing, it is a must to separate your application into distinct layers. We'll cover the basics as well as specific options to consider certain situations.

In this chapter, we will cover:

- The MVVM design pattern for code sharing
- Project and solution organization strategies
- Portable Class Libraries (PCLs)
- Preprocessor statements for platform specific code
- Dependency injection (DI) simplified
- Inversion of Control (IoC)

Learning the MVVM design pattern

The **Model-View-ViewModel** (**MVVM**) design pattern was originally invented for **WPF** (**Windows Presentation Foundation**) applications using **XAML** for separating the UI from business logic and taking full advantage of **data binding**. Applications architected in this way have a distinct ViewModel layer that has no dependencies on its user interface. This architecture in itself is optimized for unit testing as well as cross-platform development. Since an application's ViewModel classes have no dependencies on the UI layer, you can easily swap an iOS user interface for an Android one and write tests against the ViewModel layer. The MVVM design pattern is also very similar to the MVC design pattern discussed in the previous chapters.

The MVVM design pattern includes the following :

- **Model**: The model layer is the backend business logic driving the application and any business objects to go along with it. This can be anything from making web requests to a server to using a backend database.

- **View**: This layer is the actual user interface seen on the screen. In case of cross-platform development, it includes any platform-specific code for driving the user interface of the application. On iOS, this includes controllers used throughout an application and on Android, an application's activities.

- **ViewModel**: This layer acts as the glue in MVVM applications. The ViewModel layers coordinate operations between the View and Model layers. A ViewModel layer will contain properties that the view will get or set, and functions for each operation that can be made by the user on each view. The ViewModel will also invoke operations on the Model layer if needed.

The following figure shows the MVVM design pattern:

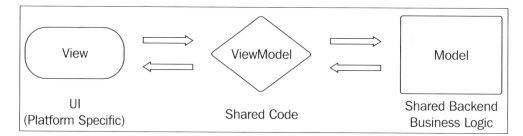

It is important to note that the interaction between the View and ViewModel layers is traditionally created by data binding with WPF. However, iOS and Android do not have built-in data binding mechanisms, so our general approach throughout the book will be to manually call the ViewModel layer from the view. There are a few frameworks out there that provide a data binding functionality such as **MVVMCross**.

To understand this pattern better, let's implement a common scenario. Let's say we have a search box on the screen and a search button. When the user enters some text and clicks on the button, a list of products and prices will be displayed to the user. In our example, we use the **async** and **await** keywords that are available in C# 5 to simplify asynchronous programming.

To implement this feature, we would start with a simple `model` class (also called a `business` object) as follows:

```
public class Product
{
   public int Id { get; set; } //Just a numeric identifier
   public string Name { get; set; } //Name of the product
   public float Price { get; set; } //Price of the product
}
```

Next, we would implement our Model layer to retrieve products based on the searched term. This is where the business logic is performed, expressing how the search needs to actually work. This is seen in the following lines of code:

```
// An example class, in the real world would talk to a web
// server or database.
public class ProductRepository
{
   // a sample list of products to simulate a database
   private Product[] products = new[]
   {
      new Product { Id = 1, Name = "Shoes", Price = 19.99m },
      new Product { Id = 2, Name = "Shirt", Price = 15.99m },
      new Product { Id = 3, Name = "Hat", Price = 9.99m },
   };

   public async Task<Product[]> SearchProducts(
      string searchTerm)
   {
      // Wait 2 seconds to simulate web request
      await Task.Delay(2000);

      // Use Linq-to-objects to search, ignoring case
      searchTerm = searchTerm.ToLower();
      return products.Where(p =>
         p.Name.ToLower().Contains(searchTerm))
         .ToArray();
   }
}
```

It is important to note here that the `Product` and `ProductRepository` classes are both considered as part of the Model layer of a cross-platform application. Some may consider `ProductRepository` as a service that is generally a self-contained class for retrieving data of some kind. It is a good idea to separate this functionality into two classes. The `Product` class's job is to hold information about a product, while `ProductRepository` is in charge of retrieving products. This is the basis for the **single responsibility principle**, which states that each class should only have one job or concern.

Next, we would implement a `ViewModel` class as follows:

```
public class ProductViewModel
{
  private readonly ProductRepository repository =
    new ProductRepository();

  public string SearchTerm
  {
    get;
    set;
  }

  public Product[] Products
  {
    get;
    private set;
  }

  public async Task Search()
  {
    if (string.IsNullOrEmpty(SearchTerm))
      Products = null;
    else
      Products = await repository.SearchProducts(SearchTerm);
  }
}
```

From here, your platform-specific code starts. Each platform would handle managing an instance of a `ViewModel` class, setting the `SearchTerm` property, and calling `Search` when the button is clicked. When the task completes, the user interface layer would update a list displayed on the screen.

If you are familiar with the MVVM design pattern used with WPF, you might notice that we are not implementing `INotifyPropertyChanged` for data binding. Since iOS and Android don't have the concept of data binding, we omitted this functionality. If you plan on having a WPF or Windows 8 version of your mobile application, you should certainly implement support for data binding where needed.

Comparing project organization strategies

You might be asking yourself at this point, how do I set up my solution in Xamarin Studio to handle shared code and also have platform-specific projects? Xamarin.iOS applications can only reference Xamarin.iOS class libraries; so, setting up a solution can be problematic. There are actually three main strategies for setting up a cross-platform solution, each with its own advantages and disadvantages.

Options for cross-platform solutions are as follows:

- **File Linking**: For this option, you would start with either a plain .NET 4.0 or .NET 4.5 class library containing all the shared code. You would then have a new project for each platform you want your app to run on. Each platform-specific project would have a subdirectory with all of the files linked in from the first class library. To set this up, add the existing files to the project, and select the **Add a link to the file** option. Any unit tests can run against the original class library. The advantages and disadvantages of file linking are as follows:
  - Advantages: This approach is very flexible. You can choose to link or not link certain files and can also use preprocessor directives such as `#if IPHONE`. You can also reference different libraries on Android versus iOS.
  - Disadvantages: You have to manage a file's existence in three projects: core library, iOS, and Android. This can be a hassle if it is a large application or if many people are working on it.

- **Cloned Project Files**: It is very similar to file linking, the main difference being that you have a class library for each platform in addition to the main project. By placing the iOS and Android projects in the same directory as the main project, the files can be added without linking. You can easily add files by right-clicking on the solution and selecting **Display Options | Show All Files**. Unit tests can run against the original class library or the platform-specific versions.
  - Advantages: This approach is just as flexible as file linking, but you don't have to manually link any files. You can still use preprocessor directives and reference different libraries on each platform.
  - Disadvantages: You still have to manage a file's existence in three projects. There is additionally some manual file arranging required to set this up. You also end up with an extra project to manage on each platform.

- **Portable Class Libraries**: This is the most optimal option; you begin the solution by making a **portable class library (PCL)** project for all your shared code. This is a special project type that allows multiple platforms to reference the same project, allowing you to use the smallest subset of C# and the .NET framework available in each platform. Each platform-specific project would reference this library directly, as well as any unit test projects.

  - Advantages: All your shared code is in one project, and all platforms use the same library. This is the cleanest and preferred approach for most cross-platform applications.

  - Disadvantages: You cannot use preprocessor directives or reference different libraries on each platform. Use of the **dependency injection** is the recommended way around this. You also could be limited to a subset of .NET depending on how many platforms you are targeting. This option has also been in beta or experimental version for some time. At the time of writing this book, PCLs are well on their way to become officially supported.

To understand each option completely and what situations call for, let's define a solution structure for each cross-platform solution. Let's use the product search example from earlier in the chapter and set up a solution for each approach.

To begin with file linking, perform the following steps:

1. Open Xamarin Studio and start a new solution.

2. Select a new **Library** project under the general **C#** section.

3. Name the project `ProductSearch.Core`, and name the solution `ProductSearch`.

4. Right-click on the newly created project and select **Options**.

5. Under **Build | General**, set the **Target Framework** option to **.NET Framework 4.5**.

6. Add the `Product`, `ProductRepository`, and `ProductViewModel` classes to the project used earlier in this chapter. You will need to add `using System.Threading.Tasks;` and `using System.Linq;` where needed.

7. Click on **Build | Build All** from the menu at the top to be sure that everything builds properly.

8. Now, let's create a new iOS project by right-clicking on the solution and selecting **Add | Add New Project**. Create a new project by navigating to **iOS | iPhone Storyboard | Single View Application** and name it `ProductSearch.iOS`.

9. Create a new Android project by right-clicking on the solution and selecting **Add | Add New Project**. Create a new project by navigating to **Android | Android Application** and name it `ProductSearch.Droid`.

10. Add a new folder named `Core` to both the iOS and Android projects.

11. Right-click on the new folder for the iOS project and select **Add | Add Files from Folder**. Select the root directory for the `ProductSearch.Core` project.

12. Check the three C# files in the root of the project. An **Add File to Folder** dialog will appear.

13. Select **Add a link to the file** and make sure the **Use the same action for all selected files** checkbox is selected.

14. Repeat this process for the Android project.

15. Click on **Build | Build All** from the menu at the top to double-check everything, and you have successfully set up a cross-platform solution with file linking.

When all is done, you will have a solution tree that looks something like what you can see in the following screenshot:

```
Solution                         □×
▼ ☐ ProductSearch
  ▼ ☐ ProductSearch.Core
    ▶ ☐ References
    ▶ ▣ Properties
      ⊞ Product.cs
      ⊞ ProductRepository.cs
      ⊞ ProductViewModel.cs
  ▼ ☐ ProductSearch.Droid
    ▶ ☐ References
      ☐ Components
    ▶ ▣ Assets
    ▼ ▣ Core
        ⊞ Product.cs
        ⊞ ProductRepository.cs
        ⊞ ProductViewModel.cs
    ▶ ▣ Properties
    ▶ ▣ Resources
      ⊞ MainActivity.cs
  ▼ ☐ ProductSearch.iOS
    ▶ ☐ References
      ☐ Components
    ▼ ▣ Core
        ⊞ Product.cs
        ⊞ ProductRepository.cs
        ⊞ ProductViewModel.cs
      ▣ Resources
      ⊞ AppDelegate.cs
      ☐ Info.plist
      ⊞ Main.cs
    ▶ ⊞ MainController.cs          ⚙▾
      ⊞ MainStoryboard.storyboard
```

You should consider using this technique when you have to reference different libraries on each platform. You might consider using this option if you are using `ReactiveUI`, `MonoGame`, or other frameworks that require you to reference a different library on iOS versus Android.

Setting up a solution with the cloned project files approach is similar to file linking, except that you will have to create an additional class library for each platform. To do this, create an Android library project and an iOS library project in the same directory: `ProductSearch.Core`. You will have to create the projects and move them to the proper folder manually, then re-add them to the solution. Right-click on the solution and select **Display Options | Show All Files** to add the required C# files to these two projects. Your main iOS and Android projects can reference these projects directly.

Your project will look like what is shown in the following screenshot, with `ProductSearch.iOS` referencing `ProductSearch.Core.iOS`, and `ProductSearch.Droid` referencing `ProductSearch.Core.Droid`:

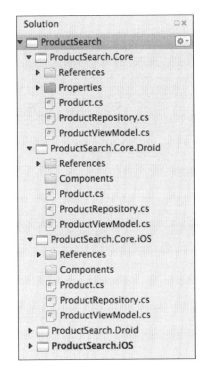

Working with portable class libraries

A **Portable Class Library** (**PCL**) is a C# library project that can be supported on multiple platforms including iOS, Android, Windows, Windows Store apps, Windows Phone, Silverlight, and Xbox 360. PCLs have been an effort by Microsoft to simplify development across different versions of the .NET framework. Xamarin has also added support for iOS and Android in the newer versions of their products. Many popular cross-platform frameworks and open source libraries are starting to develop PCL versions such as Json. NET and MVVMCross.

Let's set up a solution using PCLs. Before starting, make sure you at least have Mono 3.2.1 installed (look under **Xamarin Studio | About Xamarin Studio | Show Details**). At the time of writing this book, one could easily switch to the beta channel in Xamarin Studio to update to the version supporting PCLs.

Let's begin setting up our portable class library:

1. Open Xamarin Studio and start a new solution.

2. Select a new **Portable Library** project under the general **C#** section.

3. Name the project `ProductSearch.Core`, and name the solution `ProductSearch`.

4. Add the `Product`, `ProductRepository`, and `ProductViewModel` classes to the project used earlier in this chapter. You will need to add `using System.Threading.Tasks;` and `using System.Linq;` where needed.

5. Click on **Build | Build All** from the menu at the top to be sure everything builds properly. You may wish to remove all references this project has set, as Xamarin Studio will display them with errors (this is a known issue with PCLs).

6. Now, let's create a new iOS project by right-clicking on the solution and selecting **Add | Add New Project**. Create a new project by navigating to **iOS | iPhone Storyboard | Single View Application** and name it `ProductSearch.iOS`.

7. Create a new Android project by right-clicking on the solution and selecting **Add | Add New Project**. Create a new project by navigating to **Android | Android Application** and name it `ProductSearch.Droid`.

8. Simply add a reference to the portable class library from the iOS and Android projects.

9. Click on **Build | Build All** from the top menu and you have set up a simple solution with a portable library.

Each solution type has their distinct advantages and disadvantages. PCLs are generally better, but there are certain cases where they can't be used. For example, if you were using a library such as **MonoGame**, which is a different library for each platform, you would be much better off using file linking or cloned project files. Similar issues would arise if you needed to use a preprocessor statement such as `#if IPHONE` or a native library such as the Facebook SDK on iOS or Android.

Using preprocessor statements

When using file linking or cloned projects files, one of your most powerful tools is the use of preprocessor statements. If you are unfamiliar with them, C# has the ability to define preprocessor variables such as `#define IPHONE`, and then using `#if IPHONE` or `#if !IPHONE`.

The following is a simple example of using this technique:

```
#if IPHONE
  Console.WriteLine("I am running on iOS");
#elif ANDROID
  Console.WriteLine("I am running on Android");
#else
  Console.WriteLine("I am running on ???");
#endif
```

In Xamarin Studio, you can define preprocessor variables in your project's options under **Build** | **Compiler** | **Define Symbols**, delimited with semicolons. These will be applied to the entire project. Be warned that you must set up these variables for each configuration setting in your solution (**Debug** and **Release**); it can be an easy step to miss. You can also define these variables at the top of any C# file by declaring `#define IPHONE`, but they will only be applied within the C# file.

Let's go over another example, assuming we want to implement a class to open URLs on each platform:

```
public static class Utility
{
  public static void OpenUrl(string url)
  {
    //Open the url in the native browser
  }
}
```

The preceding example is a perfect candidate for using preprocessor statements, since it is very specific to each platform and is a fairly simple function. To implement the method on iOS and Android, we will need to take advantage of some native APIs. Refactor the class to look like the following:

```
#if IPHONE
  //iOS using statements
  using MonoTouch.Foundation;
  using MonoTouch.UIKit;
#elif ANDROID
  //Android using statements
```

```
    using Android.App;
    using Android.Content;
    using Android.Net;
#else
    //Standard .Net using statement
    using System.Diagnostics;
#endif

public static class Utility
{
  #if ANDROID
    public static void OpenUrl(Activity activity, string url)
  #else
    public static void OpenUrl(string url)
  #endif
  {
    //Open the url in the native browser
    #if IPHONE
      UIApplication.SharedApplication.OpenUrl(
        NSUrl.FromString(url));
    #elif ANDROID
      var intent = new Intent(Intent.ActionView,
        Uri.Parse(url));
      activity.StartActivity(intent);
    #else
      Process.Start(url);
    #endif
  }
}
```

The preceding class supports three different types of projects: Android, iOS, and a standard Mono or .NET framework class library. In the case of iOS, we can perform the functionality with static classes available in Apple's APIs. Android is a little more problematic, and requires an `Activity` object for launching a browser natively. We get around this by modifying the input parameters on Android. Lastly, we have a plain .NET version that uses `Process.Start()` to launch a URL. It is important to note that using the third option would not work on iOS or Android natively, which necessitates our use of preprocessor statements.

Using preprocessor statements is not normally the cleanest or the best solution for cross-platform development. They are generally best used in a tight spot or for very simple functions. Code can easily get out of hand and can become very difficult to read with many `#if` statements, so it is always better to use it in moderation. Using inheritance or interfaces is generally a better solution when a class is mostly platform specific.

Simplifying dependency injection

Dependency injection at first seems like a complex topic, but for the most part it is a simple concept. It is a design pattern aimed at making your code within your applications more flexible so that you can swap out certain functions when needed. The idea builds around setting up dependencies between classes in an application so that each class only interacts with an interface or base/abstract class. This gives you the freedom to override different methods on each platform when you need to fill in native functionality.

The concept originated from the **SOLID** object-oriented design principles, which is a set of rules you might want to research if you are interested in software architecture. The **D** in SOLID stands for **dependencies**. Specifically, the principle declares that a program should depend upon abstractions, not concretions (concrete types).

To build upon this concept, let's walk through the following example:

1. Let's assume we need to store a setting in an application that determines if the sound is on or off.

2. Now let's declare a simple interface for the setting: `interface ISettings { bool IsSoundOn { get; set; } }`.

3. On iOS, we'd want to implement this interface using the `NSUserDefaults` class.

4. Likewise, on Android, we would implement this using `SharedPreferences`.

5. Finally, any class that needs to interact with this setting would only reference `ISettings` so that the implementation could be replaced on each platform.

For reference, the full implementation of this example would look like the following snippet:

```
public interface ISettings
{
  bool IsSoundOn
  {
    get;
    set;
  }
}

//On iOS
using MonoTouch.UIKit;
using MonoTouch.Foundation;

public class AppleSettings : ISettings
```

```
{
  public bool IsSoundOn
  {
    get
    {
      return NSUserDefaults.StandardUserDefaults
      .BoolForKey("IsSoundOn");
    }
    set
    {
      var defaults = NSUserDefaults.StandardUserDefaults;
      defaults.SetBool(value, "IsSoundOn");
      defaults.Synchronize();
    }
  }
}


//On Android
using Android.Content;

public class DroidSettings : ISettings
{
  private readonly ISharedPreferences preferences;

  public DroidSettings(Context context)
  {
    preferences = context.GetSharedPreferences(
      context.PackageName, FileCreationMode.Private);
  }

  public bool IsSoundOn
  {
    get
    {
      return preferences.GetBoolean("IsSoundOn", true");
    }
    set
    {
      using (var editor = preferences.Edit())
      {
        editor.PutBoolean("IsSoundOn", value);
        editor.Commit();
      }
    }
  }
}
```

Now you would potentially have a `ViewModel` class that would only reference
`ISettings` when following the MVVM pattern. It can be seen in the following snippet:

```
public class SettingsViewModel
{
  private readonly ISettings settings;

  public SettingsViewModel(ISettings settings)
  {
    this.settings = settings;
  }

  public bool IsSoundOn
  {
    get;
    set;
  }

  public void Save()
  {
    settings.IsSoundOn = IsSoundOn;
  }
}
```

Using a ViewModel layer for such a simple example is not necessarily needed,
but you can see it would be useful if you needed to perform other tasks such as
input validation. A complete application might have a lot more settings and might
need to present the user with a loading indicator. Abstracting out your setting's
implementation has other benefits that adds flexibility to your application. Let's say
you suddenly need to replace `NSUserDefaults` on iOS with the iCloud function;
you can easily do so by implementing a new `ISettings` class and the remainder of
your code will remain unchanged. This will also help you target new platforms such
as Windows Phone, where you may choose to implement `ISettings` in a platform-
specific way.

Implementing Inversion of Control

You might be asking yourself at this point in time, how do I switch out different classes
such as the `ISettings` example? **Inversion of Control (IoC)** is a design pattern meant
to complement dependency injection and solve this problem. The basic principle is
that many of the objects created throughout your application are managed and created
by a single class. Instead of using the standard C# constructors for your `ViewModel` or
`Model` classes, a service locator or factory class would manage them throughout
the application.

There are many different implementations and styles of IoC, so let's implement a simple service locator class to use through the remainder of this book as follows:

```
public static class ServiceContainer
{
  static readonly Dictionary<Type, Lazy<object>> services =
    new Dictionary<Type, Lazy<object>>();

  public static void Register<T>(Func<T> function)
  {
    services[typeof(T)] = new Lazy<object>(() => function());
  }

  public static T Resolve<T>()
  {
    return (T)Resolve(typeof(T));
  }

  public static object Resolve(Type type)
  {
    Lazy<object> service;
    if (services.TryGetValue(type, out service)
    {
      return service.Value;
    }
    throw new Exception("Service not found!");
  }
}
```

This class is inspired by the simplicity of XNA/MonoGame's `GameServiceContainer` class, and follows the **service locator** pattern. The main differences are the heavy use of generics and the fact that it is a static class.

To use our `ServiceContainer` class, we would declare the version of `ISettings` or other interfaces that we want to use throughout our application by calling `Register` as seen in the following lines of code:

```
//iOS version of ISettings
ServiceContainer.Register<ISettings>(() => new AppleSettings());

//Android version of ISettings
ServiceContainer.Register<ISettings>(() => new DroidSettings());

//You can even register ViewModels
ServiceContainer.Register<SettingsViewModel>(() =>
  new SettingsViewModel());
```

On iOS, you could place this registration code in either your `static void Main()` method or in the `FinishedLaunching` method of your `AppDelegate` class. These methods are always called before the application is started.

On Android, it is a little more complicated. You cannot put this code in the `OnCreate` method of your activity, set as the main launcher. In some situations, the OS can close your application but restart it later in another activity. This situation is likely to cause an exception to be raised. The guaranteed safe place to put this is in a custom Android `Application` class, which has an `OnCreate` method that is called prior to any activities being created in your application. The following lines of code show the use of the `Application` class:

```
[Application]
public class Application : Android.App.Application
{
    //This constructor is required
    public Application(IntPtr javaReference, JniHandleOwnership
        transfer): base(javaReference, transfer)
    {

    }

    public override void OnCreate()
    {
        base.OnCreate();

        //IoC Registration here
    }
}
```

To pull a service out of the `ServiceContainer` class, we could rewrite the constructor of the `SettingsViewModel` class like the following lines of code:

```
public SettingsViewModel()
{
    this.settings = ServiceContainer.Resolve<ISettings>();
}
```

Likewise, you would use the generic `Resolve` method to pull out any `ViewModel` classes you would need to call from within controllers on iOS or activities on Android. This is a great, simple way to manage dependencies within your application.

There are, of course, some great open source libraries out there that implement IoC for C# applications. You might consider switching to one of them if you need more advanced features for service location, or just want to graduate to a more complicated IoC container.

Here are a few libraries that have been used with Xamarin projects:

- **TinyIoC**: https://github.com/grumpydev/TinyIoC
- **Ninject**: http://www.ninject.org/
- **MvvmCross**: https://github.com/slodge/MvvmCross includes a full MVVM framework as well as IoC
- **Simple Injector**: http://simpleinjector.codeplex.com
- **OpenNETCF.IoC**: http://ioc.codeplex.com

Summary

In this chapter, we learned about the MVVM design pattern and how it can be used to better architect cross-platform applications. We compared several project organization strategies for managing a Xamarin Studio solution containing both iOS and Android projects. We went over portable class libraries as the preferred option for sharing code and how to use preprocessor statements as a quick and dirty way to implement platform-specific code.

After completing this chapter, you should be able to speed up with several techniques for sharing code between iOS and Android applications using Xamarin Studio. Using the MVVM design pattern will help you divide your shared code between code that is platform specific. We also covered the three main options for setting up Xamarin Studio solutions and projects. You should also have a firm understanding of using the dependency injection and Inversion of Control to give your shared code access to the native APIs on each platform. In the next chapter, we will begin with writing a cross-platform application and dive into using these techniques.

4
XamChat –
a Cross-platform App

The best way to truly learn a programming skill, in our opinion, is to take on a simple project that requires you to exercise that skill. This gives new developers a project where they can focus on the concepts they are trying to learn without the overhead of fixing bugs or following customer requirements. To increase our understanding of Xamarin Studio and cross-platform development, let's develop a simple app called **XamChat** for iOS and Android.

In this chapter, we will cover the following topics:

- Our sample application concept
- The Model layer of our application
- Mocking a web service
- The ViewModel layer of our application
- Writing unit tests

Describing our sample application concept

The concept is simple: a chat application that uses a standard Internet connection as an alternative to sending text messages. There are several popular applications like this in the Apple App Store, probably due to the cost of text messaging and support for devices such as the iPod Touch or iPad. This should be a neat real-world example that could be useful for users, and will cover specific topics in developing applications for iOS and Android.

Before starting with the development, let's list the set of screens that we'll need:

- **Login / sign up**: This screen will include a standard login and sign-up process for the user
- **List of conversations**: This screen will include a button to start a new conversation
- **List of friends**: This screen will provide a way to add new friends when we start a new conversation
- **Conversation**: This screen will have a list of messages between you and another user, and an option to reply

A quick wireframe layout of the application would help us grasp a better understanding of the layout of the app. The following figure shows the set of screens to be included in your app:

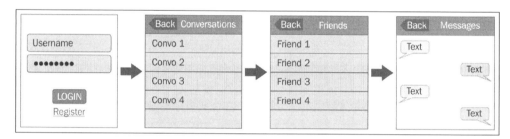

Developing our model layer

Since we have a good idea of what the application is, the next step is to develop the business objects or model layer of this application. Let's start out by defining a few classes that would contain the data to be used throughout the app. It is recommended, for the sake of organization, to add these to a `Models` folder in your project.

Let's begin with a class representing a user. The class can be created as follows:

```
public class User
{
  public int Id { get; set; }

  public string Username { get; set; }

  public string Password { get; set; }
}
```

Pretty straightforward so far; let's move on to create classes representing
a conversation and a message as follows:

```csharp
public class Conversation
{
  public int Id { get; set; }

  public int UserId { get; set; }

  public string Username { get; set; }
}

public class Message
{
  public int Id { get; set; }

  public int ConversationId { get; set; }

  public int UserId { get; set; }

  public string Username { get; set; }

  public string Text { get; set; }
}
```

Notice that we are using integers as identifiers for the various objects. UserId is
the value that would be set by the application to change the user that the object is
associated with.

Now let's go ahead and set up our solution by performing the following steps:

1. Start by creating a new solution and a new **C# Library** project.

2. Name the project as XamChat.Core and the solution as XamChat.

3. Next, let's set the library to a Mono / .NET 4.5 project. This setting is found
    in the project option dialog under **Build** | **General** | **Target Framework**.

4. You could also choose to use **Portable Library** for this project, but I've
    chosen to use a standard class library and the file-linking strategy from the
    previous chapter.

Writing a mock web service

Many times when developing a mobile application, you may need to begin the development of your application before the real backend web service is available. To prevent the development from halting entirely, a good approach would be to develop a mock version of the service. This is also helpful when you need to write unit tests, or you must wait to add a real backend to your app later.

First, let's break down the operations our app will perform against a web server. The operations are as follows:

1. Log in with a username and password.
2. Register a new account.
3. Get the user's list of friends.
4. Add friends by their usernames.
5. Get a list of the existing conversations for the user.
6. Get a list of messages in a conversation.
7. Send a message.

Now let's define an interface that offers a method for each scenario. The interface is as follows:

```
public interface IWebService
{
  Task<User> Login(string username, string password);

  Task<User> Register(User user);

  Task<User[]> GetFriends(int userId);

  Task<User> AddFriend(int userId, string username);

  Task<Conversation[]> GetConversations(int userId);

  Task<Message[]> GetMessages(int conversationId);

  Task<Message> SendMessage(Message message);
}
```

As you see, we're using asynchronous communication with the **TPL** (**Task Parallel Library**) technology.

Since communicating with a web service can be a lengthy process, it is always a good idea to use the `Task<T>` class for these operations. Otherwise, you could inadvertently run a lengthy task on the user interface thread, which would prevent user inputs during the operation. `Task` is definitely needed for web requests, since users could easily be using a cellular Internet connection on iOS and Android, and it will give us the ability to use the `async` and `await` keywords down the road.

Now let's implement a **fake** service that implements this interface. Place classes such as `FakeWebService` in the `Fakes` folder of the project. Let's start with the class declaration and the first method of the interface:

```
public class FakeWebService
{
  public int SleepDuration { get; set; }

  public FakeWebService()
  {
    SleepDuration = 1;
  }

  private Task Sleep()
  {
    return Task.Delay(SleepDuration);
  }

  public async Task<User> Login(
    string username, string password)
  {
    await Sleep();

    return new User { Id = 1, Username = username };
  }
}
```

We started off with a `SleepDuration` property to store a number in milliseconds. This is used to simulate an interaction with a web server, which can take some time. It is also useful for changing the `SleepDuration` value in different situations. For example, you might want to set this to a small number when writing unit tests so that the tests execute quickly.

Next, we implemented a simple `Sleep` method to return a task that introduce delays of a number of milliseconds. This method will be used throughout the fake service to cause a delay on each operation.

Finally, the Login method merely used an await call on the Sleep method and returned a new User object with the appropriate Username. For now, any username or password combination will work; however, you may wish to write some code here to check specific credentials.

Now, let's implement a few more methods to continue our FakeWebService class as follows:

```
public async Task<User> Register(User user)
{
  await Sleep();

  return user;
}

public async Task<User[]> GetFriends(int userId)
{
  await Sleep();

  return new[]
  {
    new User { Id = 2, Username = "bobama" },
    new User { Id = 2, Username = "bobloblaw" },
    new User { Id = 3, Username = "gmichael" },
  };
}

public async Task<User> AddFriend(
  int userId, string username)
{
  await Sleep();

  return new User { Id = 4, Username = username };
}
```

For each of these methods, we kept in mind exactly same pattern as the Login method. Each method will delay and return some sample data. Feel free to mix the data with your own values.

Now, let's implement the GetConversations method required by the interface as follows:

```
public async Task<Conversation[]> GetConversations(int userId)
{
  await Sleep();

  return new[]
  {
    new Conversation { Id = 1, UserId = 2 },
    new Conversation { Id = 1, UserId = 3 },
    new Conversation { Id = 1, UserId = 4 },
  };
}
```

Basically, we just create a new array of the Conversation objects with arbitrary IDs. We also make sure to match up the UserId values with the IDs we've used on the User objects so far.

Next, let's implement GetMessages to retrieve a list of messages as follows:

```
public async Task<Message[]> GetMessages(int conversationId)
{
  await Sleep();

  return new[]
  {
    new Message
    {
      Id = 1,
      ConversationId = conversationId,
      UserId = 2,
      Text = "Hey",
    },
    new Message
    {
      Id = 2,
      ConversationId = conversationId,
      UserId = 1,
      Text = "What's Up?",
    },
    new Message
    {
```

```
        Id = 3,
        ConversationId = conversationId,
        UserId = 2,
        Text = "Have you seen that new movie?",
      },
      new Message
      {
        Id = 4,
        ConversationId = conversationId,
        UserId = 1,
        Text = "It's great!",
      },
    };
}
```

Once again, we are adding some arbitrary data here, and mainly making sure that UserId and ConversationId match our existing data so far.

And finally, we will write one more method to send a message as follows:

```
public async Task<Message> SendMessage(Message message)
{
  await Sleep();

  return message;
}
```

Most of these methods are very straightforward. Note that the service doesn't have to work perfectly; it should merely complete each operation successfully with a delay. Each method should also return test data of some kind to be displayed in the UI. This will give us the ability to implement our iOS and Android applications while filling in the web service later.

Next, we need to implement a simple interface for persisting application settings. Let's define an interface named ISettings as follows:

```
public interface ISettings
{
  User User { get; set; }

  void Save();
}
```

Note that you might want to set up the Save method to be asynchronous and return Task if you plan on storing settings in the cloud. We don't really need this with our application since we will only be saving our settings locally.

Later on, we'll implement this interface on each platform using Android and iOS APIs. For now, let's just implement a fake version that will be used later when we write unit tests. The interface is created by the following lines of code:

```
public class FakeSettings : ISettings
{
    public User User { get; set; }

    public void Save() { }
}
```

Note that the fake version doesn't actually need to do anything; we just need to provide a class that will implement the interface and not throw any unexpected errors.

This completes the Model layer of the application. Here is a final class diagram of what we have implemented so far:

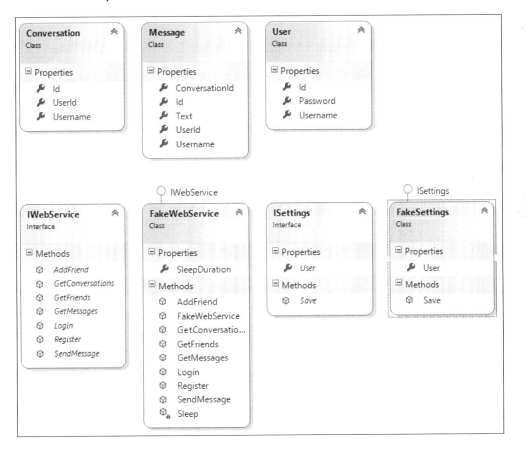

Writing the ViewModel layer

Now that we have our model layer implemented, we can move on to write the ViewModel layer. The ViewModel will be responsible for presenting each operation to the UI and offering properties to be filled out by the View layer. Other common responsibilities of this layer are input validation and simple logic to display busy indicators.

At this point, it would be a good idea to include the ServiceContainer class from the previous chapter in our XamChat.Core project, as we will be using it through our ViewModels to interact with the Model layer. We will be using it as a simple option to support dependency injection and Inversion of Control; however, you may use another library of your preference for this.

Normally, we start off by writing a base class for all the ViewModel layers within our project. This class always has the functionality shared by all the classes. It's a good place to put some parts of the code that are used by all the methods in the classes; for example, notification changes, methods, or similar instances.

Place the following code snippet in a new ViewModels folder within your project:

```
public class BaseViewModel
{
  protected readonly IWebService service =
    ServiceContainer.Resolve<IWebService>();
  protected readonly ISettings settings =
    ServiceContainer.Resolve<ISettings>();

  public event EventHandler IsBusyChanged = delegate { };

  private bool isBusy = false;

  public bool IsBusy
  {
    get { return isBusy; }
    set
    {
      isBusy = value;
      IsBusyChanged(this, EventArgs.Empty);
    }
  }
}
```

The `BaseViewModel` class is a great place to insert any common functionality that you plan on reusing throughout your application. For this app, we only need to implement some functionality to indicate if the ViewModel layer is busy. We provided a property and an event that the UI will be able to subscribe to and display a wait indicator on the screen. We also added some fields for the services that will be needed. Another common feature that could be added would be validation for user inputs; however, we don't really need it for this application.

Implementing our LoginViewModel class

Now that we have a base class for all of the ViewModel layers, we can implement ViewModel for the first screen in our application, the **Login** screen.

Now let's implement a `LoginViewModel` class as follows:

```
public class LoginViewModel : BaseViewModel
{
  public string Username { get; set; }

  public string Password { get; set; }

  public async Task Login()
  {
    if (string.IsNullOrEmpty(Username))
      throw new Exception("Username is blank.");

    if (string.IsNullOrEmpty(Password))
      throw new Exception("Password is blank.");

    IsBusy = true;
    try
    {
      settings.User = await service
        .Login(Username, Password);
      settings.Save();
    }
    finally
    {
      IsBusy = false;
    }
  }
}
```

In this class, we implemented the following:

- We subclassed `BaseViewModel` to get access to `IsBusy` and the fields containing common services
- We added the `Username` and `Password` properties to be set by the View layer
- We added a `User` property to be set when the log in process is completed
- We implemented a `Login` method to be called from View, with validation on `Username` and `Password` properties
- We set `IsBusy` during the call to the `Login` method on `IWebService`
- We set the `User` property by awaiting the result from `Login` on the web service

Basically, this is the pattern that we'll follow for the rest of the ViewModels in the application. We provide properties for the View layer to be set by the user's input, and methods to call for various operations. If it is a method that could take some time, such as a web request, you should always return `Task` and use the `async` and `await` keywords.

> Note that we used a `try` and `finally` block for setting `IsBusy` back to `false`. This will ensure it gets reset properly even when an exception is thrown. We plan on handling the error in the View layer, so we can display a native pop up to the user displaying a message.

Implementing our RegisterViewModel class

Since we have finished writing our `ViewModel` class to log in, we will now need to create one for the user's registration.

Let's implement another ViewModel to register a new user:

```
public class RegisterViewModel : BaseViewModel
{
  public string Username { get; set; }

  public string Password { get; set; }

  public string ConfirmPassword { get; set; }
}
```

These properties will handle inputs from the user. Next, we need to add a `Register` method as follows:

```
public async Task Register()
{
  if (string.IsNullOrEmpty(Username))
    throw new Exception("Username is blank.");

  if (string.IsNullOrEmpty(Password))
    throw new Exception("Password is blank.");

  if (Password != ConfirmPassword)
    throw new Exception("Passwords don't match.");

  IsBusy = true;
  try
  {
    settings.User = await service
      .Register(new User { Username = Username,
        Password = Password, });
    settings.Save();
  }
  finally
  {
    IsBusy = false;
  }
}
```

The `RegisterViewModel` class is very similar to the `LoginViewModel` class, but has an additional `ConfirmPassword` property for the UI to set. A good rule to follow for when to split up the ViewModel layer's functionality is to always create a new class when the UI has a new screen. This helps to keep your code clean and somewhat follow the **single responsibility principle** for your classes. This concept states that a class should only have a single purpose or responsibility. We'll try to follow this concept to keep our classes small and organized, which can be more important than usual when sharing code across platforms.

Implementing our FriendViewModel class

Next on the list is a ViewModel layer to work with a user's friend list. We will need a method to load a user's friend list and add a new friend.

Now let's implement the `FriendViewModel` as follows:

```
public class FriendViewModel : BaseViewModel
{
  public User[] Friends { get; private set; }

  public string Username { get; set; }
}
```

Now we'll need a method to load friends. This method is as follows:

```
public async Task GetFriends()
{
  if (settings.User == null)
    throw new Exception("Not logged in.");

  IsBusy = true;
  try
  {
    Friends = await service
      .GetFriends(settings.User.Id);
  }
  finally
  {
    IsBusy = false;
  }
}
```

Finally, we'll need a method to add a new friend, and then update the list of friends contained locally:

```
public async Task AddFriend()
{
  if (settings.User == null)
    throw new Exception("Not logged in.");

  if (string.IsNullOrEmpty(Username))
    throw new Exception("Username is blank.");

  IsBusy = true;
  try
```

```
{
    var friend = await service
        .AddFriend(settings.user.Id, Username);

//Update our local list of friends
    var friends = new List<User>();
    if (Friends != null)
        friends.AddRange(Friends);
    friends.Add(friend);

    Friends = friends
        .OrderBy(f => f.Username)
            .ToArray();
    }
    finally
    {
        IsBusy = false;
    }
}
```

Again, this class is fairly straightforward. The only thing new here is that we added some logic to update the list of friends and sort them within our client application and not the server. You could also choose to reload the complete list of friends if you have a good reason to do so.

Implementing our MessageViewModel class

Our final required ViewModel layer will be handling messages and conversations. We need to create a way to load conversations and messages, and send a new message.

Let's start implementing our MessageViewModel class as follows:

```
public class MessageViewModel : BaseViewModel
{
    public Conversation[] Conversations { get; private set; }

    public Conversation Conversation { get; set; }

    public Message[] Messages { get; private set; }

    public string Text { get; set; }
}
```

Next, let's implement a method to retrieve a list of conversations as follows:

```
public async Task GetConversations()
{
  if (settings.User == null)
    throw new Exception("Not logged in.");

  IsBusy = true;
  try
  {
    Conversations = await service
      .GetConversations(settings.User.Id);
  }
  finally
  {
    IsBusy = false;
  }
}
```

Similarly, we need to retrieve a list of messages within a conversation. We will need to pass the conversation ID to the service as follows:

```
public async Task GetMessages()
{
  if (Conversation == null)
    throw new Exception("No conversation.");

  IsBusy = true;
  try
  {
    Messages = await service
      .GetMessages(Conversation.Id);
  }
  finally
  {
    IsBusy = false;
  }
}
```

Finally, we need to write some code to send a message and update the local list of messages as follows:

```
public async Task SendMessage()
{
  if (settings.User == null)
    throw new Exception("Not logged in.");

  if (Conversation == null)
    throw new Exception("No conversation.");

  if (string.IsNullOrEmpty (Text))
    throw new Exception("Message is blank.");

  IsBusy = true;
  try
  {
    var message = await service.SendMessage( new Message
{
  UserId = settings.User.Id,
  ConversationId = Conversation.Id,
  Text = Text,
});

//Update our local list of messages
    var messages = new List<Message>();
    if (Messages != null)
      messages.AddRange(Messages);
    messages.Add(message);

    Messages = messages.ToArray();
  }
  finally
  {
    IsBusy = false;
  }
}
```

This concludes the ViewModel layer of our application and the entirety of the shared code used on iOS and Android. For the `MessageViewModel` class, you could have also chosen to put `GetConversations` and `Conversations` properties in their own class, since they could be considered as a separate responsibility, but it is not really necessary.

Here is the final class diagram of our ViewModel layer:

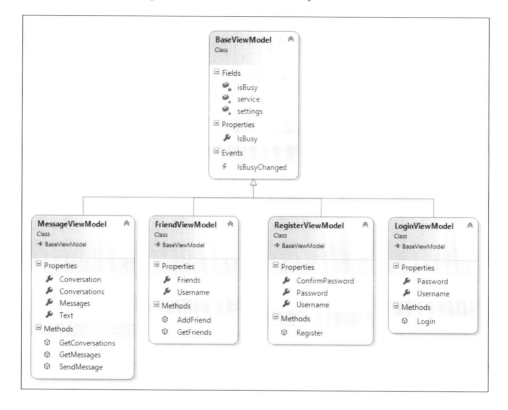

Writing unit tests

Since all the code we've written so far is not dependent on the user interface, we can easily write unit tests against our classes. This step is generally taken after the first implementation of a `ViewModel` class. Proponents of **Test Driven Development (TDD)** would recommend writing tests first and implementing things afterward, so choose which method is best for you. In either case, it is a good idea to write tests against your shared code before you start using them from the View layer, so you catch bugs before they hold up your development on the UI.

Xamarin projects take advantage of an open source testing framework called **NUnit**. It was originally derived from a Java testing framework called **JUnit**, and is the de facto standard for unit testing C# applications. Xamarin Studio provides several project templates for writing tests with **NUnit**.

Setting up a new project for unit tests

Let's set up a new project for unit tests by performing the following steps:

1. Add a new **NUnit Library** project to your solution, found under the **C#** section.

2. Name the project as XamChat.Tests to keep things consistent.

3. Next, let's set the library to a Mono/.NET 4.5 project under the project options, then **Build | General | Target Framework**.

4. Right-click on the project references and choose **Edit References**.

5. Under the **Projects** tab, add a reference to **XamChat.Core**.

6. Now, open the Test.cs file and notice the following required attributes that make up a unit test using NUnit:

     ○ using NUnit.Framework;: This attribute is the main statement to be used to work with NUnit

     ○ [TestFixture]: This decorates a class to indicate that the class has a list of methods for running tests

     ○ [Test]: This decorates a method to indicate a test

In addition to the required C# attributes, there are several others that are useful for writing tests and they are as follows:

- [TestFixtureSetUp]: This decorates a method that runs before all the tests contained within a text fixture class.

- [SetUp]: This decorates a method that runs before each test in a test fixture class.

- [TearDown]: This decorates a method that runs after each test in a test fixture class.

- [TestFixtureTearDown]: This decorates a method that runs after all the tests in a text fixture class have been completed.

- [ExpectedException]: This decorates a method that is intended to throw an exception. It is useful to test cases that are supposed to fail.

- [Category]: This decorates a test method and can be used to organize different tests; for example, you might categorize fast and slow tests.

Writing assertions

The next concept to learn about writing tests with NUnit is learning how to write **assertions**. An assertion is a method that will throw an exception if a certain value is not true. It will cause a test to fail and give a descriptive explanation as to what happened. NUnit has a couple of different sets of APIs for assertions; however, we will use the more readable and fluent version of the APIs.

The basic syntax of fluent-style API is using the `Assert.That` method. The following example shows the use of the method:

```
Assert.That(myVariable, Is.EqualTo(0));
```

Likewise, you can assert the opposite:

```
Assert.That(myVariable, Is.Not.EqualTo(0));
```

Or any of the following:

- `Assert.That(myVariable, Is.GreaterThan(0));`
- `Assert.That(myBooleanVariable, Is.True);`
- `Assert.That(myObject, Is.Not.Null);`

Feel free to explore the APIs. With code completion in Xamarin Studio, you should be able to discover useful static members or methods on the `Is` class to use within your tests.

Before we begin writing specific tests for our application, let's write a static class and method to create a global setup to be used throughout our tests; you can rewrite `Test.cs` as follows:

```
public static class Test
{
  public static void SetUp()
  {
    ServiceContainer.Register<IWebService>(() =>
      new FakeWebService {SleepDuration = 0, });
    ServiceContainer.Register<ISettings>(() =>
      new FakeSettings());
  }
}
```

We'll use this method throughout our tests to set up fake services in our Model layer. Additionally, this replaces the existing services so that our tests execute against new instances of these classes. This is a good practice in unit testing to guarantee that no old data is left behind from a previous test. Also notice that we set `SleepDuration` to `0`. This will make our tests run very quickly.

Begin by creating a `ViewModels` folder in your test's project and adding a class named `LoginViewModelTests` as follows:

```
public class LoginViewModelTests
{
    LoginViewModel loginViewModel;
    ISettings settings;

    [SetUp]
    public void SetUp()
    {
        Test.SetUp();

        settings = ServiceContainer.Resolve<ISettings>();
        loginViewModel = new LoginViewModel();
    }

    [Test]
    public void LoginSuccessfully()
    {
        loginViewModel.Username = "testuser";
        loginViewModel.Password = "password";

        loginViewModel.Login().Wait();

        Assert.That(settings.User, Is.Not.Null);
    }
}
```

Notice our use of a `SetUp` method. We recreate the objects used in every test to make sure that no old data is left over from the previous test runs. Another point to note is that there is currently no support for `async`/`await` in NUnit (although it will be supported in NUnit 2.6.2). To work around this, we call the `Wait` method directly on any methods that return `Task` or `Task<T>`.

To run the test, use the NUnit menu found docked to the right of Xamarin Studio by default. Go ahead and run the test by using the **Run Test** button that has a gear icon; you should get a successful result similar to what is shown in the following screenshot:

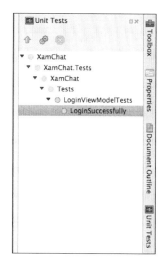

You can also view the **Test Results** pane, which will show extended details if a test fails, as shown in the following screenshot:

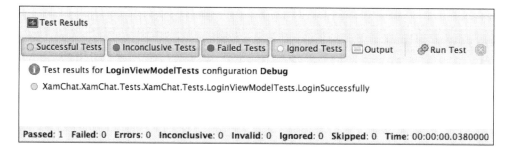

To see what happens when a test fails, go ahead and modify your test to assert against an incorrect value as follows:

```
//Change Is.Not.Null to Is.Null
Assert.That(settings.User, Is.Null);
```

You will get a very descriptive error in the **Test Results** pane as shown in the following screenshot:

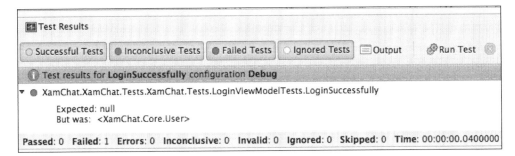

Now let's implement another test for the `LoginViewModel` class; let's make sure we get the appropriate outcome if the username and password is blank. The test is implemented as follows:

```
[Test]
public void LoginWithNoUsernameOrPassword()
{
    //Throws an exception
    loginViewModel.Login.Wait();
}
```

If we run the test as is, we will get an exception and the test will fail. Since we expect an exception to occur, we can decorate the method to make the test pass only if an exception occurs as follows:

```
[Test, ExpectedException(typeof(AggregateException))]
```

> Note that an `AggregateException` type is thrown if a task fails its execution. You can also set the `ExpectedMessage` property on the attribute if you wish to check for a specific error message.

More tests are included with the sample code along with this book. It is recommended to write tests against each public operation on each `ViewModel` class. Additionally, write tests for any validation or other important business logic. I would also recommend writing tests against the Model layer; however, it is not needed in our project yet since we only have fake implementations.

Summary

In this chapter, we went over the concept for a sample application that we will be building throughout this book called XamChat. We also implemented the core business objects for the application in the Model layer. Since we do not have a server to support this application yet, we implemented a fake web service. This gives us the flexibility to move forward with the app without building a server application. We also implemented the ViewModel layer. This layer will expose operations in a simple way to the View layer. Finally, we wrote tests covering the code we've written so far using NUnit. Writing tests against shared code in a cross-platform application can be very important, as it is the backbone of more than one application.

After reading this chapter, you should have completed the shared library for our cross-platform application in its entirety. You should have a very firm grasp on our application's architecture and its distinct Model and ViewModel layers. You should also have a good understanding on how to write fake versions of parts of your application that you may not be ready to implement quite yet. In the next chapter, we will implement the iOS version of XamChat.

5
XamChat for iOS

To begin writing the iOS version of XamChat, create a new **Single View Application** under the **iOS** section of the **New Project** dialog. Name the project XamChat.iOS or some other appropriate name of your choice. The project template will automatically create a controller with an unfamiliar name; go ahead and delete it. We will create our own controllers as we go.

In this chapter, we will cover the following:

- The basics of an iOS application
- The use of UINavigationController
- Implementing a login screen
- Segues and UITableView
- Adding a friends list
- Adding a list of messages
- Composing messages

Understanding the basics of an iOS app

Before we start developing our app, let's review the main settings of the application. Apple uses a file named Info.plist to store important information about any iOS app. These settings are used when an iOS application is installed on a device by the Apple App Store. Begin development on any new iOS application by editing this file.

Xamarin Studio provides a useful menu to modify values in the `Info.plist` file, as shown in the following screenshot:

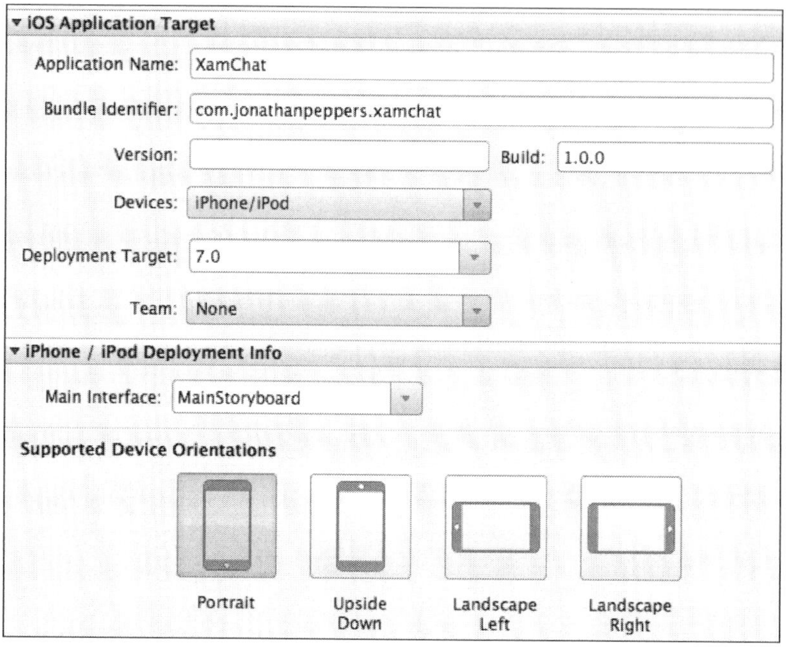

The most important settings are as follows:

- **Application Name**: This is the title below an app's icon in iOS. Note that this is not the same as the official name of your app in the iOS App Store.
- **Bundle Identifier**: This is your app's bundle identifier or bundle ID. It is a unique name to identify your application. The convention is to use reverse domain naming style beginning with your company name, such as `com.packt.xamchat`.
- **Version**: This is a version number for your application such as `1.0.0`.
- **Devices**: In this you can select **iPhone/iPod**, **iPad**, or **Universal** (all devices) for your application.
- **Deployment Target**: This is the minimum iOS version your application runs on.
- **Main Interface**: This is the main storyboard file for your app.
- **Supported Device Orientations**: These are the different positions your application will be able to rotate to and support.

There are other settings for app icons, splash screens, and so on. You can also toggle between the **Advanced** or **Source** tabs to configure additional settings that Xamarin does not provide a user-friendly menu for.

Configure the following settings for our application:

- **Application Name**: XamChat
- **Bundle Identifier**: com.yourcompanyname.xamchat; make sure you name future apps beginning with com.yourcompanyname
- **Version**: This can be any version number you prefer; it should not be left blank
- **Devices**: **iPhone/iPod**
- **Deployment Target**: **7.0**
- **Supported Device Orientations**: Only select **Portrait**

You can find some additional settings for Xamarin iOS applications if you right-click on your project and select **Options**, as shown in the following screenshot. It is a good idea to know what is available for iOS-specific projects in Xamarin Studio.

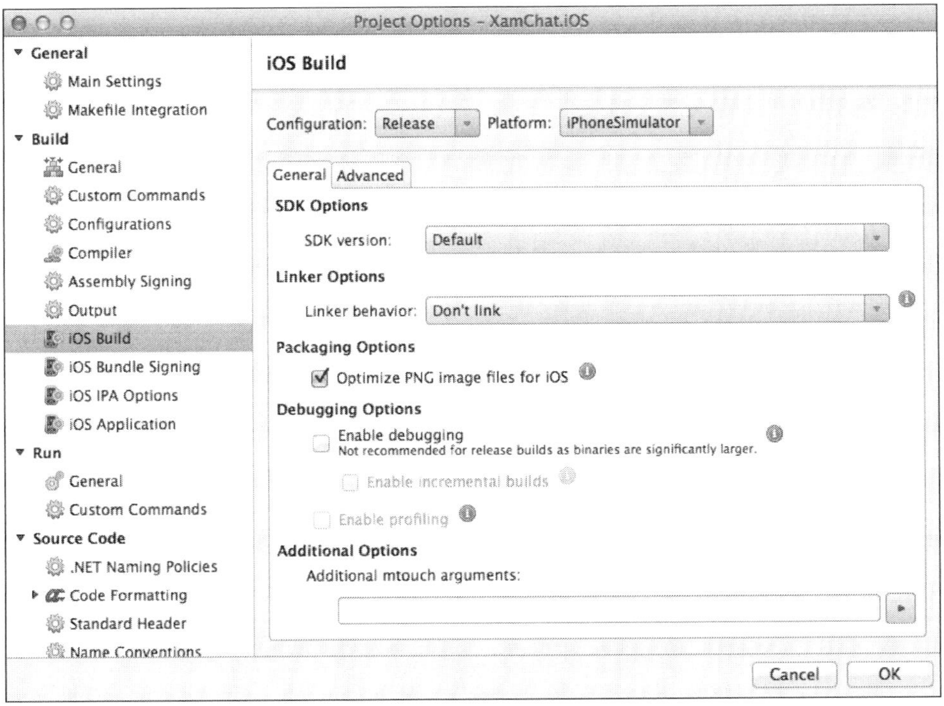

Let's discuss some of the following most important options:

- **iOS Build**
  - ◦ **SDK version**: This is the version of the iOS SDK to compile your application with. It is generally best to use **Default**.
  - ◦ **Linker behavior**: Xamarin has implemented a feature called **linking**. The linker will strip any code that will never be called within your assemblies. This keeps your application small and allows them to ship a stripped-down version of the core Mono framework with your app. In most cases, it is best to use the **Link SDK assemblies only** option. We will cover linking in the next chapter.
  - ◦ **Optimize PNG files for iOS**: Apple uses a custom PNG format to speed up the loading of PNGs within your app. You can turn this off to speed up builds, or if you plan on optimizing the images yourself.
  - ◦ **Enable debugging**: Turning this on allows Xamarin to include extra information with your app to enable debugging from Xamarin Studio.
  - ◦ **Additional mtouch arguments**: This field is for passing extra command-line arguments to the Xamarin compiler for iOS. You can check the complete list of these arguments at `http://iosapi.xamarin.com`.

- **iOS Build | Advanced**
  - ◦ **Supported architectures**: Here, the options are **ARMv7**, **ARMv7s**, and a **FAT** version that includes both. These are instruction sets that different iOS device processors support. If you really care about performance, you might consider selecting the option to support both; however, this will make your application larger.
  - ◦ **Use LLVM optimizing compiler**: Checking this compiles code in such a way that is smaller and runs faster, but takes longer to compile. **LLVM** stands for **Low Level Virtual Machine**.
  - ◦ **Enable generic value type sharing**: This is an option specific to Mono that draws better performance from C# generics with value types. It has the downside of making the application slightly larger, but I would recommend leaving it on.
  - ◦ **Use SGen generational garbage collector**: This uses the new Mono garbage collector in your app. I would recommend turning this on if you really need good performance with the **garbage collector** (**GC**) or are working on an app that needs to be responsive in real time, such as a game.

- **iOS Bundle Signing**
  - **Identity**: This is the certificate to identify the app's creator for deploying the application to devices. We'll cover more on this in later chapters.
  - **Provisioning profile**: This is a specific profile that deploys the app to a device. This works in tandem with Identity, but also declares the distribution method, the devices that can install the app, and other specific declarations for the app such as iCloud or push notifications.

- **iOS Application**: These settings are identical to what you see in the `Info.plist` file.

For this application, you can leave all these options at their defaults. When making a real iOS application on your own, you should consider changing many of these as per your application's needs.

Using UINavigationController

In iOS applications, the key class for managing navigation between different controllers is the `UINavigationController` class. It is a parent controller that contains several child controllers in a stack. Users can move forward by putting new controllers on top of the stack or using a built-in back button to pop a controller off the stack and navigate to the previous screen.

The developer can manipulate the navigation controller's stack with the following methods:

- `SetViewControllers`: This sets an array of child controllers. It has a value to optionally animate the transition.
- `ViewControllers`: This is a property for getting or setting the array of child controllers without an option for animations.
- `PushViewController`: This places a new child controller at the top of the stack with an option to display an animation.
- `PopViewControllerAnimated`: This pops off the child controller at the top of the stack with an option to animate the transition.
- `PopToViewController`: This pops children off the stack until reaching the specified child controller, removing all controllers above it. It provides an option to animate the transition.
- `PopToRootViewController`: This removes all child controllers except the bottom-most controller. It includes an option to display an animation.
- `TopViewController`: This is a property that returns the child controller that is currently on top of the stack.

It is important to note that using the option for animations will cause a crash if you try to modify the stack during the animation. To fix this situation, either use the `SetViewControllers` method and set the entire list of child controllers, or refrain from using the animations during a combination of transitions.

Let's set up a navigation controller in our application by performing the following steps:

1. Double-click on the `MainStoryboard.storyboard` file to open it in Xcode.
2. Remove the controller that was created by the project template.
3. On the bottom-right of the dialog, drag a **Navigation Controller** element onto the storyboard.
4. Remove the **Table View Controller** element that was created automatically.
5. Drag a new **View Controller** element next to Navigation Controller.
6. Right-click and drag the **Navigation Controller** element to the new **View Controller** element. You will first see a blue line appear and then a pop up when you release.
7. Under **Relationship Segue**, select **root view controller**.
8. You will see a **segue** that connects the two controllers. We'll cover this concept in more detail later in the chapter.
9. Save the storyboard file and return to Xamarin Studio.

If you run the application at this point, you will have a basic iOS app with a status bar at the top, a navigation controller containing a navigation bar, and a child controller that is completely white, as shown in the following screenshot:

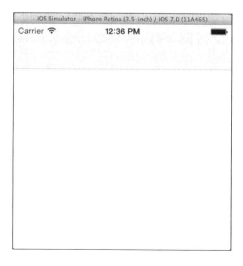

Implementing the login screen

Since the first screen of our application will be a login screen, let's begin by setting up the appropriate views in the storyboard file. We will implement the login screen by using Xamarin Studio to write the C# code, and Xcode for creating iOS layouts in our storyboard file.

Return to the project in Xamarin Studio and perform the following steps:

1. Double-click on the `MainStoryboard.storyboard` file to open it in Xcode.

2. Select your view controller and click on the **Identity Inspector** tab. It is the third tab from the left, located on the right-hand side of the screen.

3. Under the **Custom Class** section, enter `LoginController` into the **Class** field.

4. Save the file and return to Xamarin Studio. Notice that the `LoginController` class is generated for you. You may create a `Controllers` folder and move the file in it if you wish.

The following screenshot shows what the controller's settings will look like in Xcode after the changes have been made:

Now let's modify the layout of the controller by performing the following steps:

1. Double-click on the `MainStoryboard.storyboard` file a second time to return to Xcode.

2. Drag two text fields onto the controller. Position and size them appropriately for the username and password entries.

3. For the second field, check the **Secure** checkbox under the **Text Field** section. This will set the control to hide the characters for the password field.

4. Drag a button onto the controller. Rename the button as `Login`.

5. Drag an activity indicator onto the controller. Check the **Animating** and **Hidden** checkboxes.

6. Create an outlet for each of the controls. Toggle on the **Assistant Editor** by selecting the button in the top-right corner of Xcode that resembles a tuxedo, as shown in the following screenshot:

7. You may have to select the `LoginController.h` header file in the upper navigation of the code window.

8. Next, create the outlets by right-clicking and dragging from each control to the header file. In the pop up that appears, name the outlets `username`, `password`, `login`, and `indicator` respectively.

9. Save the header and storyboard files and return to Xamarin Studio.

Your outlet set up in the storyboard will look something like what is shown in the following screenshot:

```
// WARNING
// This file has been generated automatically by Xamarin Studio
     to
// mirror C# types. Changes in this file made by drag-
     connecting
// from the UI designer will be synchronized back to C#, but
// more complex manual changes may not transfer correctly.


#import <Foundation/Foundation.h>
#import <UIKit/UIKit.h>

@interface LoginController : UIViewController {
    UIActivityIndicatorView *_indicator;
    UIButton *_login;
    UITextField *_password;
    UITextField *_username;
}

@property (nonatomic, retain) IBOutlet UIActivityIndicatorView
    *indicator;

@property (nonatomic, retain) IBOutlet UIButton *login;

@property (nonatomic, retain) IBOutlet UITextField *password;

@property (nonatomic, retain) IBOutlet UITextField *username;

@end
```

XamChat

Username

Password

Login

Go ahead and compile the application to make sure everything is okay. At this point, we need to add all of our code from the shared library to the project using the file-linking strategy. Create a new folder in the `XamChat.iOS` project named `Core`. Right-click and go to **Add | Add Files From Folder**, and add all the files from the `XamChat.Core` project. You will now be able to access all the shared code we wrote in the previous chapter.

Next let's set up our iOS application to register all its view models and other services that will be used throughout the application. We will use the `ServiceContainer` class we created in *Chapter 4, XamChat – a Cross-platform App*, to set up dependencies throughout our application. Open `AppDelegate.cs` and add the following method:

```
public override bool FinishedLaunching(
  UIApplication application,
  NSDictionary launchOptions)
{
  //View Models
  ServiceContainer.Register<LoginViewModel>(() =>
    new LoginViewModel());
  ServiceContainer.Register<FriendViewModel>(() =>
    new FriendViewModel());
  ServiceContainer.Register<RegisterViewModel>(() =>
    new RegisterViewModel());
  ServiceContainer.Register<MessageViewModel>(() =>
    new MessageViewModel());

  //Models
  ServiceContainer.Register<ISettings>(() =>
    new FakeSettings());
  ServiceContainer.Register<IWebService>(() =>
    new FakeWebService());
}
```

Down the road, we will replace the fake services with real ones. Now let's add the login functionality to `LoginController.cs`. First add `LoginViewModel` to a member variable at the top of the class as follows:

```
readonly LoginViewModel loginViewModel =
  ServiceContainer.Resolve<LoginViewModel>();
```

This will pull a shared instance of `LoginViewModel` into a local variable in the controller. This is the pattern we will use throughout the book in order to pass a shared view model from one class to another.

le `ViewDidLoad` to hook up the view model's functionality with the
in outlets as follows:

```
override void ViewDidLoad()

    ViewDidLoad();

login.TouchUpInside += async(sender, e) =>
{
  loginViewModel.Username = username.Text;
  loginViewModel.Password = password.Text;

  try
  {
    await loginViewModel.Login();

    //TODO: navigate to a new screen
  }
  catch (Exception exc)
  {
    new UIAlertView("Oops!", exc.Message, null, "Ok").Show();
  }
};
}
```

We'll add the code to navigate to a new screen later in the chapter.

Next, let's hook up the `IsBusyChanged` event to actually perform an action as follows:

```
public override void ViewWillAppear()
{
  base.ViewWillAppear();

  loginViewModel.IsBusyChanged += OnIsBusyChanged;
}

public override void ViewWillDisappear()
{
  base.ViewWillDisappear();

  loginViewModel.IsBusyChanged -= OnIsBusyChanged;
}

void OnIsBusyChanged(object sender, EventArgs e)
{
```

```
    username.Enabled =
      password.Enabled =
      login.Enabled =
      indicator.Hidden = !loginViewModel.IsBusy;
}
```

Now you might ask, why do we subscribe to the event in this manner? The problem is that the `LoginViewModel` class will exist through your application's lifetime, while the `LoginController` class will not. If we subscribed to the event in `ViewDidLoad` but didn't unsubscribe from it later, then our application would have a memory leak. We also avoided using a lambda expression for the event, since it would otherwise be impossible to unsubscribe the event. Note that we don't have the same problem with the `TouchUpInside` event on the button, since it will live in memory the same amount of time as the controller does. This is a common problem with events in C#, which is why it is a good idea to use the preceding pattern on iOS.

If you run the application now, you should be able to enter a username and password, as shown in the following screenshot. On pressing **Login**, you should see the indicator appear and all the controls disabled. Your application will call the shared code correctly, and should function correctly when we add a real web service.

Using segues and UITableView

A segue is a transition from one controller to another. In the same way, a storyboard file is a collection of controllers and their views attached together by segues. This in turn allows you to see the layouts of each controller and the general flow of your application at the same time.

There are just a few categories of segue, which are as follows:

- **Push**: This is used within a navigation controller. It pushes a new controller to the top of the navigation controller's stack. Push uses the standard animation on iOS for navigation controllers and is generally the most commonly used segue.

- **Relationship**: This is used to set a child controller of another controller. For example, the root controller of a navigation controller, container views, or split view controllers in an iPad application.

- **Modal**: On using this, a controller presented modally will appear on top of the parent controller. It will cover the entire screen until dismissed. There are several types of different transition animations available.

- **Custom**: This is a custom segue that includes an option for a custom class, which subclasses `UIStoryboardSegue`. This gives you fine-grained control over the animation and how the next controller is presented.

Segues also follow the following pattern while executing:

- The destination controller and its views are created.

- The segue object, a subclass of `UIStoryboardSegue`, is created. This is normally only important for custom segues.

- The `PrepareForSegue` method is called on the source controller. This is a good place to run any custom code before a segue begins.

- The segue's `Perform` method is called and the transition animation is started. This is where the bulk of the code resides for a custom segue.

In Xcode you have the choice of either firing a segue automatically from a button or table view row, or just giving the segue an identifier. In the second case, you can start the segue yourself by calling the `PerformSegue` method on the source controller by using its identifier.

Now let's set up a new segue by setting up some aspects of our `MainStoryboard.storyboard` file, by performing the following steps:

1. Double-click on the `MainStoryboard.storyboard` file to open it in Xcode.

2. Add a new **Table View Controller** to the storyboard.

3. Select your view controller and click on the **Identity Inspector** tab. It is the third tab from the left, located on the right-hand side of the screen.

4. Under the **Custom Class** section, enter `ConversationsController` into the **Class** field.

5. Create a segue from `LoginController` to `ConversationsController` by right-clicking and dragging the blue line from one controller to the other.

6. Select the **push** segue from the pop up that appears.

7. Select the segue by clicking on it and give it an identifier of `OnLogin`. You'll find this under the **Attributes Inspector** tab on the right-hand side of the screen.

8. Save the storyboard file and return to Xamarin Studio.

Open `LoginController.cs`, and modify the line of code that we marked as `TODO` earlier in this chapter as follows:

```
PerformSegue("OnLogin", this);
```

Now if you build and run the application, you will navigate to the new controller after a successful log in. The segue will be performed, and you will see the built-in animation provided by the navigation controller.

Next, let's set up the table view on the second controller. We are using a powerful class on iOS called `UITableView`. It is used in many situations and is very similar to the concept of a list view on other platforms. The `UITableView` class is controlled by another class called `UITableViewSource`. It has methods that you need to override to set up how many rows should exist and how those rows should be displayed on the screen.

> Note that `UITableViewSource` is a combination of `UITableViewDelegate` and `UITableViewDataSource`. I prefer to use `UITableViewSource` for simplicity, since many times using both of the other two classes would be required.

Before we jump in and start coding, let's review the most commonly used methods on `UITableViewSource`, which are as follows:

- `RowsInSection`: This method allows you to define the number of rows in a section. All table views have a number of sections and rows. By default, there is only one section; however, it is a requirement to return the number of rows in a section.

- `NumberOfSections`: This is the number of sections in the table view.

- `GetCell`: This method must return a cell for each row. It is up to the developer to set up what a cell should look like; you can also implement code to recycle the cells as you scroll. Recycling cells will yield better performance while scrolling.

- `TitleForHeader`: This method, if overridden, is the simplest way to return a string for the title. Each section in a table view can has a standard header view by default.

- `RowSelected`: This method will be called when the user selects a row.

There are additional methods that you can override, but these will get you by in most situations. You can also set up custom headers and footers if you need to develop a custom styled table view.

Now let's open the `ConversationsController.cs` file, and create a nested class inside `ConversationsController` as follows:

```
class TableSource : UITableViewSource
{
  const string CellName = "ConversationCell";
  readonly MessageViewModel messageViewModel =
    ServiceContainer.Resolve<MessageViewModel>();

  public override int RowsInSection(
    UITableView tableView, int section)
  {
    return messageViewModel.Conversations == null ?
      0 : messageViewModel.Conversations.Length;
  }

  public override UITableViewCell GetCell(
    UITableView tableView, NSIndexPath indexPath)
  {
    var conversation =
      messageViewModel.Conversations[indexPath.Row];
    var cell = tableView.DequeueReusableCell(CellName);
    if (cell == null)
    {
      cell = new UITableViewCell(
        UITableViewCellStyle.Default, CellName);
      cell.Accessory =
        UITableViewCellAccessory.DislosureIndicator;
    }
    cell.TextLabel.Text = conversation.Username;
    return cell;
  }
}
```

We implemented the two required methods for setting up a table view: RowsInSection and GetCell. We returned the number of conversations found on the view model and set up our cell for each row. We also used UITableViewCellAccessory.DislosureIndicator to add an indicator for the users know they can click on the row.

Notice our implementation of recycling cells. Calling DequeueReusableCell with a cell identifier will return a null cell the first time around. If null, you should create a new cell using the same cell identifier. Subsequent calls to DequeueReusableCell will return an existing cell if available, enabling you to reuse it. You can also define UITableView cells in the storyboard file, which is useful for custom cells. Our cell here is very simple, so it is easier to define it from C# code. Recycling cells is important on mobile platforms to preserve memory and provide the user with a very fluid scrolling table.

Next, we need to set up the TableView source on TableView. Add some changes to our ConversationsController class as follows:

```
readonly MessageViewModel messageViewModel =
  ServiceContainer.Resolve<MessageViewModel>();

public override void ViewDidLoad()
{
  base.ViewDidLoad();

  TableView.Source = new TableSource();
}

public async override void ViewWillAppear()
{
  base.ViewWillAppear ();

  try
  {
    await messageViewModel.GetConversations();

    TableView.ReloadData();
  }
  catch(Exception exc)
  {
    new UIAlertView("Oops!", exc.Message, null, "Ok").Show();
  }
}
```

So when the view appears, we will load our list of conversations. Upon completion of that task, we'll reload the table view so that it displays our list of conversations. If you run the application, you'll see a few conversations appear in the table view after logging in, as shown in the following screenshot. Down the road, everything will operate in the same manner when we load the conversations from a real web service.

Adding a friends list screen

The next fairly important screen is that of our friends list. When creating a new conversation, the app will load a list of friends to start a conversation with. We'll follow a very similar pattern to load our list of conversations.

To begin, we'll create `UIBarButtonItem` which navigates to a new controller named `FriendsController`, by performing the following steps:

1. Double-click on the `MainStoryboard.storyboard` file to open it in Xcode.

2. Add a new **Table View Controller** to the storyboard.

3. Select your view controller and click on the **Identity Inspector** tab. It is the third tab from the left, located on the right-hand side of the screen.

4. Under the **Custom Class** section, enter `FriendsController` into the **Class** field.

5. Create a new **Bar Button Item** element and place on the top-right of the navigation bar of the `ConversationsController` class.

6. In the **Attributes Inspector** of the bar button, set its **Identifier** to **Add**. This will use the built-in plus button, which is commonly used throughout iOS applications.

7. Create a segue from **Bar Button Item** to the `FriendsController` by right-clicking and dragging the blue line from the bar button to the next controller.

8. Select the **push** segue from the pop up that appears.

9. Save the storyboard file and return to Xamarin Studio.

You should see a new `FriendsController` class that Xamarin Studio has generated for you. If you compile and run the application, you'll see the new bar button item we've created. Clicking on it will navigate you to the new controller.

Now let's implement `UITableViewSource` to display our friends list. Start with a new nested class inside `FriendsController` as follows:

```
class TableSource : UITableViewSource
{
  const string CellName = "FriendCell";
  readonly FriendViewModel friendViewModel =
    ServiceContainer.Resolve<FriendViewModel>();

  public override int RowsInSection(
    UITableView tableView, int section)
  {
    return friendViewModel.Friends == null ?
      0 : friendViewModel.Friends.Length;
  }

  public override UITableViewCell GetCell(
    UITableView tableView, NSIndexPath indexPath)
  {
    var friend = friendViewModel.Friends[indexPath.Row];
    var cell = tableView.DequeueReusableCell(CellName);
    if (cell == null)
    {
      cell = new UITableViewCell(
        UITableViewCellStyle.Default, CellName);
      cell.AccessoryView =
        UIButton.FromType(UIButtonType.ContactAdd);
      Cell.AccessoryView.UserInteractionEnabled = false;
    }
    cell.TextLabel.Text = friend.Username;
    return cell;
  }
}
```

Just as before, we implemented table cell recycling and merely set the text on the label for each friend. We used `cell.AccessoryView` to indicate to the user that each cell is clickable and starts a new conversation. We disabled user interaction on the button just to allow the row to be selected when the user clicks on the button. Otherwise, we'd have to implement a click event for the button.

Next, we'll need to modify `FriendsController` in the same way as we did for conversations as follows:

```
readonly FriendViewModel friendViewModel =
  ServiceContainer.Resolve<FriendViewModel>();

public override void ViewDidLoad()
{
  base.ViewDidLoad();

  TableView.Source = new TableSource();
}

public async override void ViewWillAppear()
{
  base.ViewWillAppear ();

  try
  {
    await friendViewModel.GetFriends();

    TableView.ReloadData();
  }
  catch(Exception exc)
  {
    new UIAlertView("Oops!", exc.Message, null, "Ok").Show();
  }
}
```

This will function exactly as the conversations list; the controller will load the friends list asynchronously and refresh the table view. If you compile and run the application, you'll be able to navigate to the screen and view the sample friend list we created in *Chapter 4, XamChat – a Cross-platform App*, as shown in the following screenshot:

Adding a list of messages

Now let's implement the screen to view a conversation or list of messages. We will try to model the screen after the built-in text message application on iOS. To do so, we will also cover the basics of how to create custom table view cells.

To start, we'll need a new `MessagesController` class, so perform the following steps:

1. Double-click on the `MainStoryboard.storyboard` file to open it in Xcode.

2. Add a new **Table View Controller** to the storyboard.

3. Select your view controller and click on the **Identity Inspector** tab. It is the third tab from the left, located on the right-hand side of the screen.

4. Under the **Custom Class** section, enter `MessagesController` into the **Class** field.

5. Create a segue from `ConversationsController` to `MessagesController` by right-clicking and dragging the blue line from the bar button to the next controller.

6. Select the **push** segue from the pop up that appears. Name the segue `OnConversation` by using **Attributes Inspector**.

7. Now create two **Table View Cell** onto the table view in `MessagesController`. You may reuse the existing one created by default.

8. Using the **Custom Class** section, enter `MyMessageCell` and `TheirMessageCell` respectively into the **Class** field for each cell.

9. Switch to the **Attributes Inspector** and set **Identifier** to `MyCell` and `TheirCell`.

10. Save the storyboard file and return to Xamarin Studio.

Xamarin Studio will generate three files: `MessagesController.cs`, `MyMessageCell.cs`, and `TheirMessageCell.cs`. You might decide to keep things organized by creating a `Views` folder and moving the cells into it. Likewise, you can move the controller to a `Controllers` folder.

Now let's implement a base class for both cells to inherit from:

```
publi class BaseMessageCell : UITableViewCell
{
  public BaseMessageCell(IntPtr handle) : base(handle)
  {
  }
  public virtual void Update(Message message)
  {
  }
}
```

We will override the `Update` method later and take the appropriate action for each cell type. We need this class to make things easier while interacting with both types of cells from `UITableViewSource`.

Now open `MessagesController.cs` and implement `UITableViewSource` inside a nested class as follows:

```
class TableSource : UITableViewSource
{
  const string MyCellName = "MyCell";
  const string TheirCellName = "TheirCell";
  readonly MessageViewModel messageViewModel =
    ServiceContainer.Resolve<MessageViewModel>();
  readonly ISettings settings =
    ServiceContainer.Resolve<ISettings>();
  public override int RowsInSection(
    UITableView tableview, int section)
  {
    return messageViewModel.Messages == null ?
      0 : messageViewModel.Messages.Length;
  }
  public override UITableViewCell GetCell(
    UITableView tableView, NSIndexPath indexPath)
  {
    var message = messageViewModel.Messages [indexPath.Row];
```

```
    bool isMyMessage = message.UserId == settings.User.Id;
    var cell = tableView.DequeueReusableCell(isMyMessage ?
      MyCellName : TheirCellName) as BaseMessageCell;
    cell.Update(message);
    return cell;
  }
}
```

We added some logic to check if a message is from a current user to decide on the appropriate table cell identifier. Since we have a base class for both cells, we can cast to BaseMessageCell and use its Update method.

Now let's make the required changes to our MessagesController as follows:

```
readonly MessageViewModel messageViewModel =
  ServiceContainer.Resolve<MessageViewModel>();
public override void ViewDidLoad()
{
  base.ViewDidLoad();
  TableView.Source = new TableSource(this);
}
public async override void ViewWillAppear(bool animated)
{
  base.ViewWillAppear(animated);

  Title = messageViewModel.Conversation.Username;
  try
  {
    await messageViewModel.GetMessages();
    TableView.ReloadData();
  }
  catch (Exception exc)
  {
    new UIAlertView("Oops!", exc.Message, null, "Ok").Show();
  }
}
```

The only thing new here is where we set the Title property to the username of the conversation.

To complete our custom cells, we will need to make more changes in Xcode by performing the following steps:

1. Double-click on the MainStoryboard.storyboard file to open it in Xcode.
2. Drag a new **Label** onto both the custom cells.

3. Use some creativity to style both labels. I chose to make the text in MyMessageCell blue and TheirMessageCell green. I set **Alignment** on the label to the right aligned in TheirMessageCell.

4. Make an outlet for the label in both cells, and name it message. You will need to make sure you select the appropriate MyMessageCell.h and TheirMessageCell.h file for each of the cell in Xcode.

5. Save the storyboard file and return to Xamarin Studio.

Now add the following Update method to both MyMessageCell.cs and TheirMessageCell.cs:

```
public partial class MyMessageCell : BaseMessageCell
{
  public MyMessageCell (IntPtr handle) : base (handle)
  {
  }
  public override void Update(Message message)
  {
    this.message.Text = message.Text;
  }
}
```

It is a bit strange to have duplicated the code for each cell, but it is the simplest approach to take advantage of the outlets Xamarin Studio generated based on the storyboard file. You could also have chosen to use the same class for both cells (even with a different layout in Xcode); however, you then lose the ability to have different code in each cell.

If you run the application now, you will be able to view the messages list. The following screenshot shows my version in which I chose to add a date and time to the messages as well:

Composing messages

For the final piece of our application, we need to implement custom functionality that Apple doesn't provide with their APIs. We need to add a text field with a button that appears to be attached to the bottom of the table view. Most of this will require writing code and wiring up a lot of events.

Let's begin by adding some new member variables to our `MessagesController` class as follows:

```
UIToolbar toolbar;
UITextField message;
UIBarButtonItem send;
NSObject willShowObserver, willHideObserver;
```

We will place the text field and bar buttons inside the toolbar, as in the following code. The `NSObject` fields will be an example of iOS's event system called **notifications**. We'll see how those are used shortly.

```
public override void ViewDidLoad()
{
  base.ViewDidLoad();
  //Text Field
  message = new UITextField(new RectangleF(0, 0, 240, 32))
  {
    BorderStyle = UITextBorderStyle.RoundedRect,
    ReturnKeyType = UIReturnKeyType.Send,
    ShouldReturn = _ =>
    {
      Send();
      return false;
    },
  };

  //Bar button item
  send = new UIBarButtonItem("Send", UIBarButtonItemStyle.Plain,
    (sender, e) => Send());
  //Toolbar
  toolbar = new UIToolbar(
    new RectangleF(0, TableView.Frame.Height - 44,
    TableView.Frame.Width, 44));
  toolbar.Items = new UIBarButtonItem[]
  {
    new UIBarButtonItem(message),
    send
  };
```

```
        NavigationController.View.AddSubview(toolbar);
        TableView.Source = new TableSource();
        TableView.TableFooterView = new UIView(
          new RectangleF(0, 0, TableView.Frame.Width, 44))
        {
          BackgroundColor = UIColor.Clear,
        };
      }
```

Much of this work is basic UI setup. It is not something we can do inside Xcode, because it is a custom UI in this case. We create a text field, bar button item, and toolbar from C# and add them to our navigation controller's view. This will display the toolbar at the top of the table view, no matter where it is scrolled to. Another trick we used was to add a footer view to the table view, which is of the same height as the toolbar. This will simplify some animations that we'll set up later.

Now we will need to modify ViewWillAppear as follows:

```
      public async override void ViewWillAppear(bool animated)
      {
        base.ViewWillAppear(animated);
        Title = messageViewModel.Conversation.Username;
        //Keyboard notifications
        willShowObserver = UIKeyboard.Notifications.ObserveWillShow(
          (sender, e) => OnKeyboardNotification(e));
        willHideObserver = UIKeyboard.Notifications.ObserveWillHide(
          (sender, e) => OnKeyboardNotification(e));
        //IsBusy
        messageViewModel.IsBusyChanged += OnIsBusyChanged;
        try
        {
          await messageViewModel.GetMessages();
          TableView.ReloadData();
          message.BecomeFirstResponder();
        }
        catch (Exception exc)
        {
          new UIAlertView("Oops!", exc.Message, null, "Ok").Show();
        }
      }
```

Most of these changes are straightforward, but notice our use of iOS notifications. Xamarin has provided a C# friendly way to subscribe to notifications. There is a static nested class named Notifications inside various UIKit classes that provide notifications. Otherwise, you would have to use the NSNotificationCenter class, which is not as easy to use. To unsubscribe from these events, we merely need to dispose NSObject that is returned.

So let's add an override for `ViewWillDisapper` to clean up these events as follows:

```
public override void ViewWillDisappear(bool animated)
{
  base.ViewWillDisappear(animated);
  //Unsubcribe notifications
  if (willShowObserver != null)
  {
    willShowObserver.Dispose();
    willShowObserver = null;
  }
  if (willHideObserver != null)
  {
    willHideObserver.Dispose();
    willHideObserver = null;
  }
  //IsBusy
  messageViewModel.IsBusyChanged -= OnIsBusyChanged;
}
```

Next, let's set up our methods for these events as follows:

```
void OnIsBusyChanged (object sender, EventArgs e)
{
  message.Enabled =
    send.Enabled = !messageViewModel.IsBusy;
}

void ScrollToEnd()
{
  TableView.ContentOffset = new PointF(
    0, TableView.ContentSize.Height -
    TableView.Frame.Height);
}

void OnKeyboardNotification (UIKeyboardEventArgs e)
{
  //Check if the keyboard is becoming visible
  bool willShow = e.Notification.Name ==
    UIKeyboard.WillShowNotification;
  //Start an animation, using values from the keyboard
  UIView.BeginAnimations("AnimateForKeyboard");
  UIView.SetAnimationDuration(e.AnimationDuration);
  UIView.SetAnimationCurve(e.AnimationCurve);
  //Calculate keyboard height, etc.
```

```
  if (willShow)
  {
    var keyboardFrame = e.FrameEnd;
    var frame = TableView.Frame;
    frame.Height -= keyboardFrame.Height;
    TableView.Frame = frame;
    frame = toolbar.Frame;
    frame.Y -= keyboardFrame.Height;
    toolbar.Frame = frame;
  }
  else
  {
    var keyboardFrame = e.FrameBegin;
    var frame = TableView.Frame;
    frame.Height += keyboardFrame.Height;
    TableView.Frame = frame;
    frame = toolbar.Frame;
    frame.Y += keyboardFrame.Height;
    toolbar.Frame = frame;
  }
  //Commit the animation
  UIView.CommitAnimations();
  ScrollToEnd();
}
```

That is quite a bit of code, but not too difficult. OnIsBusyChanged is used to disable some of our views while it is loading. ScrollToEnd is a quick method to scroll the table view to the end. We need this for the sake of usability. Some math is required because Apple does not provide a built-in method for this.

On the other hand, OnKeyboardNotification has quite a lot going on. We used the built-in animation system for iOS to set up an animation when the keyboard appears or hides. We use this to move views around for the on-screen keyboard. Using the animation system is quite easy; call UIView.BeginAnimations, modify some views, and then finish up with UIView.CommitAnimations. We also used a few more values from the keyboard to time our animation identically with the keyboard's animations.

Last but not least, we need to implement a function for sending a new message as follows:

```
async void Send()
{
  //Just hide the keyboard if they didn't type anything
  if (string.IsNullOrEmpty(message.Text))
```

```
{
    message.ResignFirstResponder();
    return;
}
//Set the text, send the message
messageViewModel.Text = message.Text;
await messageViewModel.SendMessage();
//Clear the text field & view model
message.Text =
    messageViewModel.Text = string.Empty;
//Reload the table
TableView.ReloadData();
//Hide the keyboard
message.ResignFirstResponder();
//Scroll to end, to see the new message
ScrollToEnd();
}
```

This code is also fairly straightforward. After sending the message, we merely need to reload the table, hide the keyboard, and then make sure we scroll to the bottom to see the new message, as shown in the following screenshot. Using the async keyword makes this easy.

Summary

In this chapter, we covered the basic settings that Apple and Xamarin provide for developing iOS applications. This includes the `Info.plist` file and project options in Xamarin Studio. We covered `UINavigationController`, the basic building block for navigation in iOS applications, and implemented a login screen complete with username and password fields. Next, we covered iOS segues and the `UITableView` class. We implemented the friends list screen using `UITableView`, and the messages list screen, also using `UITableView`. Lastly, we added a custom UI functionality: a custom toolbar floating at the bottom of the messages list.

Upon completing this chapter, you will have a partially functional iOS version of XamChat. You will have a deeper understanding of the iOS platform and tools, and fairly good knowledge to apply to building your own iOS applications. Take it upon yourself to implement the remaining screens that we did not cover in the chapter. If you get lost, feel free to review the full sample application included with this book.

6
XamChat for Android

To begin writing the Android version of XamChat, open the solution provided in the previous chapters and create a new **Android Application** project. Name the project XamChat.Droid or some other appropriate name of your choice.

In this chapter, we will cover:

- The Android manifest
- Writing a login screen for XamChat
- Android's ListView and BaseAdapter
- Adding a friends list
- Adding a list of messages

Introducing Android Manifest

All Android applications the have an XML file called the Android Manifest, which declares basic information about the app, and is named AndroidManifest.xml. This is very similar to the Info.plist file on iOS, but Android puts much more emphasis on its importance. A default project doesn't have a manifest, so begin creating one by going to **Project Options | Android Application** and clicking on **Add Android Manifest**. Several new settings for your application will appear.

The most important settings are as follows:

- **Application name**: This is the title of your application, which is displayed below the icon. It is not the same as the name selected on Google Play.
- **Package name**: This is just like on iOS; it's your app's bundle identifier or bundle ID. It is a unique name to identify your application. The convention is to use the reverse domain style with your company name at the beginning, for example, com.packt.xamchat. It must begin with a lower case letter and contain at least one . character within.

- **Application icon**: This is the icon displayed for your app on Android's home screen.

- **Version number**: This is a one-digit number that represents the version of your application. Raising this number indicates a newer version on Google Play.

- **Version name**: This is a user-friendly version string for your app, for example, **1.0.0**.

- **Minimum Android version**: This is the minimum version of Android that your application supports.

- **Target Android version**: This is the version of the Android SDK your application is compiled against. Using higher numbers gives you access to new APIs; however, you might need to do some checks to prevent calling these APIs on older devices.

- **Install Location**: This defines the different locations your Android application can be installed to: auto (user settings), external (SD card), or internal (device internal memory).

These settings are shown as follows:

In addition to these settings, there is a set of checkboxes labeled **Required permissions**. These are displayed to users on Google Play prior to the application being installed. This is Android's way of enforcing a level of security, giving users a way to see what kinds of access an app will have to make changes to their device.

The following are some commonly used manifest permissions:

- **Camera**: This provides access to the device camera
- **Internet**: This provides access to make web requests over the internet
- **ReadContacts**: This provides access to read the device's contacts library
- **ReadExternalStorage**: This provides access to read the SD card
- **WriteContacts**: This provides access to modify the device's contacts library
- **WriteExternalStorage**: This provides access to write to the SD card

In addition to these settings, a manual change to Android Manifest will be required many times. In this case, you can edit the manifest file as you would a standard XML file in Xamarin Studio. For a complete list of valid XML elements and attributes, visit `http://developer.android.com/guide/topics/manifest/manifest-intro.html`.

Now let's fill out the following settings for our application:

- **Application name**: `XamChat`
- **Package name**: `com.yourcompanyname.xamchat`; make sure to name future apps beginning with `com.yourcompanyname`
- **Version number**: Just start with the number `1`
- **Version**: This can be any string, but it is recommended to use something resembling a version number
- **Minimum Android version**: Select **Android 4.0.3 (API Level 15)**
- **Required permissions**: Select **Internet**; we will be using it later

At this point, we need to add all of our code from the shared library to the project using the **file-linking** strategy. Create a new folder in the `XamChat.Droid` project named `Core`. Right-click, then click on **Add | Add Files From Folder** and add all the files from the `XamChat.Core` project. You will now be able to access all the shared code that was written in *Chapter 4, XamChat – a Cross-platform App*. Additionally, any changes we make to the core code will be made to the original files to keep everything in sync.

Go to the `Resources` directory, and in the `values` folder open `Strings.xml`; this is where all the text throughout your Android app should be stored. This is an Android convention that will make it very easy to add multiple languages to your application.

Let's change our strings to the following:

```xml
<?xml version="1.0" encoding="utf-8"?>
<resources>
  <string name="ApplicationName">XamChat</string>
  <string name="ErrorTitle">Oops!</string>
  <string name="Loading">Loading</string>
</resources>
```

We'll use these values later in the chapter; feel free to add new ones in cases where you display text to the user.

Now let's implement our main application class; add a new **Android Class** from the **New File** dialog. This is the same as the standard class template, but it adds several Android-using statements to the top of the file that imports the Android APIs to be used within your code. Create a new `Application` class where we can register everything in our `ServiceContainer` as follows:

```csharp
[Application(Theme = "@android:style/Theme.Holo.Light")]
public class Application : Android.App.Application
{
  public Application(
    IntPtr javaReference, JniHandleOwnership transfer)
    : base(javaReference, transfer)
  {

  }

  public override void OnCreate()
  {
    base.OnCreate();

    //ViewModels
    ServiceContainer.Register<LoginViewModel>(
      () => new LoginViewModel());
    ServiceContainer.Register<FriendViewModel>(
      () => new FriendViewModel());
    ServiceContainer.Register<MessageViewModel>(
      () => new MessageViewModel());
    ServiceContainer.Register<RegisterViewModel>(
      () => new RegisterViewModel());

    //Models
    ServiceContainer.Register<ISettings>(
      () => new FakeSettings());
```

```
        ServiceContainer.Register<IWebService>(
          () => new FakeWebService());
    }
}
```

We used the built-in Android theme, `Theme.Holo.Light`, just because it is a neat theme that matches the default style we used on iOS.

Now let's implement a simple base class for all the activities throughout our app. Create an `Activities` folder in the `XamChat.Droid` project and a new file named `BaseActivity.cs` with the following contents:

```
[Activity]
public class BaseActivity<TViewModel> : Activity
  where TViewModel : BaseViewModel
{
  protected readonly TViewModel viewModel;
  protected ProgressDialog progress;

  public BaseActivity()
  {
    viewModel = ServiceContainer.Resolve(typeof(TViewModel)) as
      TViewModel;
  }

  protected override void OnCreate(Bundle bundle)
  {
    base.OnCreate(bundle);

    progress = new ProgressDialog(this);
    progress.SetCancelable(false);
    progress.SetTitle(Resource.String.Loading);
  }

  protected override void OnResume()
  {
    base.OnResume();
    viewModel.IsBusyChanged += OnIsBusyChanged;
  }

  protected override void OnPause()
  {
    base.OnPause();
    viewModel.IsBusyChanged -= OnIsBusyChanged;
  }
```

```
    void OnIsBusyChanged (object sender, EventArgs e)
    {
      if (viewModel.IsBusy)
        progress.Show();
      else
        progress.Hide();
    }
  }
```

We did several things here to simplify the development of our other activities. First, we made this class generic, and made a protected variable named `viewModel` to store a view model of a specific type. Note that we did not use generics on controllers in iOS due to platform limitations (see more on Xamarin's documentation website at `http://docs.xamarin.com/guides/ios/advanced_topics/limitations/`). We also implemented `IsBusyChanged`, and displayed a simple `ProgressBar` function with the `Loading` string from the `Strings.xml` file to indicate network activity.

Let's add one more method for displaying errors to the user as follows:

```
    protected void DisplayError(Exception exc)
    {
      string error = exc.Message;
      new AlertDialog.Builder(this)
        .SetTitle(Resource.String.ErrorTitle)
        .SetMessage(error)
        .SetPositiveButton(Android.Resource.String.Ok,
          (IDialogInterfaceOnClickListener)null)
        .Show();
    }
```

This method will display a pop-up dialog indicating that something went wrong. Notice we also used `ErrorTitle` and the built-in Android resource for an `Ok` string.

This will complete the core setup for our Android application. From here, we can move on to implement the UI for the screens throughout our app.

Adding a login screen

Before creating Android views, it is important to know the different layouts or view group types available in Android. iOS does not have an equivalent for some of these because iOS has a very small variation of screen sizes on its devices. Since Android has virtually infinite screen sizes and densities, the Android SDK has a lot of built-in support for auto-sizing and layout for views.

The following are the common types of layout:

- `ViewGroup`: This is the base class for a view that contains a collection of child views. You normally won't use this class directly.

- `LinearLayout`: This is a layout that positions its child views in rows or columns (but not both). You can also set weights on each child to have them span different percentages of the available space.

- `RelativeLayout`: This is a layout that gives much more flexibility on the position of its children. You can position child views relative to each other so that they are above, below, to the left, or to the right of one another.

- `FrameLayout`: This layout positions its child views directly on top of one another in the **z order** on the screen. This layout is best used for cases where you have a large child view that needs other views on top of it and perhaps docked to one side.

- `ListView`: This displays views vertically in a list with the help of an adapter class that determines the number of child views. It also has support for its children to be selected.

- `GridView`: This displays views in rows and columns within a grid. It also requires the use of an adapter class to supply the number of children.

Before we begin writing the login screen, delete the `Main.axml` and `MainActivity.cs` files that were created from the Android project template. Next, create an Android layout file named `Login.axml` in the `layout` folder of the `Resources` directory in your project.

Now we can start adding functionalities to our Android layout as follows:

1. Double-click on the new layout file to open the Android designer.
2. Drag two **Plain Text** views onto the layout found in the **Text Fields** section.
3. In the **Id** field, enter `@+id/username` and `@+id/password` respectively.
4. For the password field, set its **Input Type** property to `textPassword`.
5. Drag a **Button** onto the layout and set its **Text** property to `Login`.
6. Set the button's **Id** property to `@+id/login`.

Your layout will look something like the following screenshot when complete:

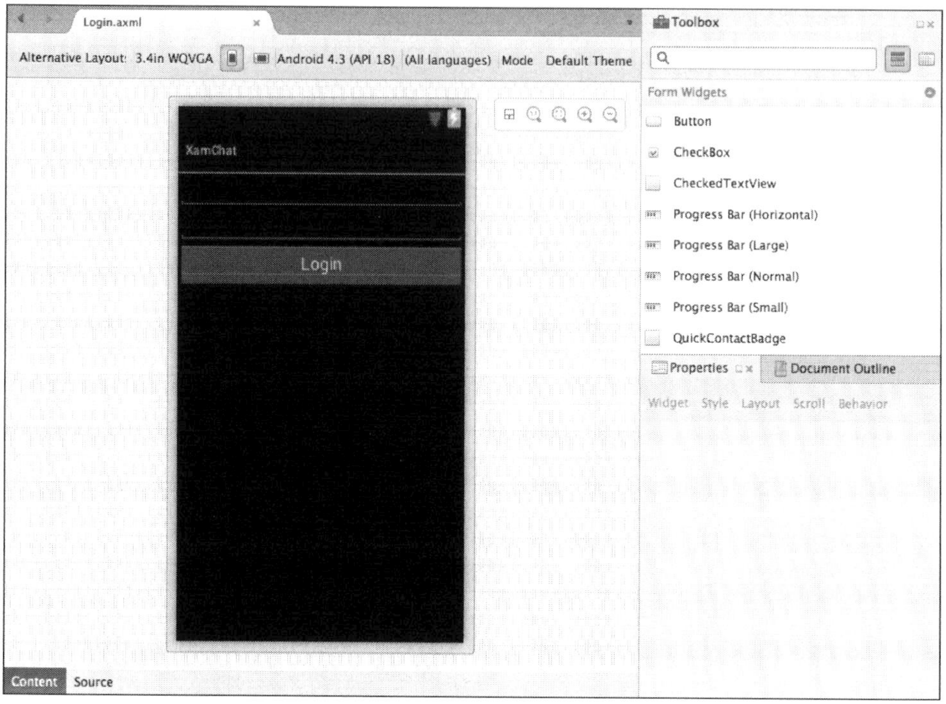

Now create a new Android Activity file named `LoginActivity.cs` in the `Activities` folder we created earlier. Let's implement the login functionality as follows:

```
[Activity(Label = "@string/ApplicationName", MainLauncher = true)]
public class LoginActivity : BaseActivity<LoginViewModel>
{
  EditText username, password;
  Button login;

  protected override void OnCreate(Bundle bundle)
  {
    base.OnCreate(bundle);
    SetContentView(Resource.Layout.Login);
    username = FindViewById<EditText>(Resource.Id.username);
    password = FindViewById<EditText>(Resource.Id.password);
    login = FindViewById<Button>(Resource.Id.login);
    login.Click += OnLogin;
  }
```

```
protected override void OnResume()
{
  base.OnResume();
  username.Text =
    password.Text = string.Empty;
}
async void OnLogin (object sender, EventArgs e)
{
  viewModel.Username = username.Text;
  viewModel.Password = password.Text;
  try
  {
    await viewModel.Login();
    //TODO: navigate to a new activity
  }
  catch (Exception exc)
  {
    DisplayError(exc);
  }
}
}
```

Notice that we set `MainLauncher` to `true` to make this activity the first activity for the application. We also took advantage of the `ApplicationName` value and `BaseActivity` class we set up earlier in the chapter. We also overrode `OnResume` to clear out the two `EditText` controls so that the values are cleared out if you return to the screen.

Now if you launch the application, you will be greeted by the login screen we just implemented, as shown in the following screenshot:

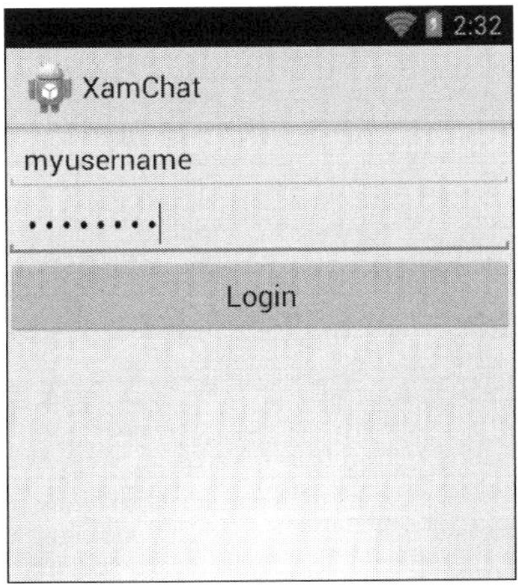

Using ListView and BaseAdapter

Now let's implement a conversations list on Android. The Android equivalent of `UITableView` and `UITableViewSource` are `ListView` and `BaseAdapter`. There are parallel concepts for these Android classes compared to iOS, such as implementing abstract methods and recycling cells during scrolling. There are a few different types of adapters used in Android such as `ArrayAdapter` or `CursorAdaptor`, although `BaseAdapter` is generally best suited for simple lists.

Let's implement our conversations screen. Begin by making a new Android Activity in your `Activities` folder named `ConversationsActivity.cs`. Let's start with only a couple of changes to the class definition as follows:

```
[Activity(Label = "Conversations")]
public class ConversationsActivity :
  BaseActivity<MessageViewModel>
{
  //Other code here later
}
```

Perform the following steps to implement a couple of Android layouts:

1. Create a new Android Layout in the `layout` folder of the `Resources` directory named `Conversations.axml`.

2. Drag a **ListView** control from **Toolbox** onto the layout and set its **Id** field to `@+id/conversationsList`.

3. Create a second Android Layout; the `layout` folder in the `Resources` directory named `ConversationListItem.axml`.

4. Drag a **Medium Text** and a **Small Text** control onto the layout from the **Toolbox**.

5. Set their IDs to `@+id/conversationUsername` and `@+id/conversationLastMessage`.

6. Finally, let's set each of their **Margins** fields to `3dp` in the **Layout** tab of the **Properties** box.

This will set up all the layout files we'll need to use throughout the conversations screen.

Now we can implement `BaseAdapter` as a nested class inside of `ConversationsActivity` as follows:

```
class Adapter : BaseAdapter<Conversation>
{
  readonly MessageViewModel messageViewModel =
```

```
      ServiceContainer.Resolve<MessageViewModel>();
    readonly LayoutInflater inflater;
    public Adapter(Context context)
    {
      inflater = (LayoutInflater)context.GetSystemService (
        Context.LayoutInflaterService);
    }
    public override long GetItemId(int position)
    {
      return messageViewModel.Conversations [position].Id;
    }
    public override View GetView(
      int position, View convertView, ViewGroup parent)
      {
        if (convertView == null)
        {
          convertView = inflater.Inflate (
            Resource.Layout.ConversationListItem, null);
        }
      var conversation = this [position];
      var username = convertView.FindViewById<TextView>(
        Resource.Id.conversationUsername);
      var lastMessage = convertView.FindViewById<TextView>(
        Resource.Id.conversationLastMessage);
      username.Text = conversation.Username;
      lastMessage.Text = conversation.LastMessage;
      return convertView;
    }
    public override int Count
    {
      get { return messageViewModel.Conversations == null ? 0
        : messageViewModel.Conversations.Length; }
    }
    public override Conversation this[int index]
    {
      get { return messageViewModel.Conversations [index]; }
    }
  }
```

The following is a review of what is going on inside the adapter:

- We subclassed BaseAdapter<Conversation>.

- We passed in a Context parameter (our activity) so that we can pull out the LayoutInflater. This class enables us to load XML layout resources and inflate them into a view object.

- We implemented `GetItemId`. This is a general method used to identify rows, so try to return a unique number.

- We set up `GetView`, which recycles the `convertView` variable by only creating a new view if it is null. We also pulled out the text views in our layout to set their text.

- We overrode `Count` to return the number of conversations.

- We implemented an indexer to return a `Conversation` object for a position.

Overall, this should be fairly similar to what we did on iOS.

Now let's set up the adapter in our activity by adding the following to the body of `ConversationsActivity`:

```
ListView listView;
Adapter adapter;
protected override void OnCreate(Bundle bundle)
{
  base.OnCreate(bundle);
  SetContentView(Resource.Layout.Conversations);
  listView = FindViewById<ListView>(
    Resource.Id.conversationsList);
  listView.Adapter =
    adapter = new Adapter(this);
}
protected async override void OnResume()
{
  base.OnResume();
  try
  {
    await viewModel.GetConversations();
    adapter.NotifyDataSetInvalidated();
  }
  catch (Exception exc)
  {
    DisplayError(exc);
  }
}
```

This code will set up the adapter and reload our list of conversations when the activity appears on screen. Note that we called `NotifyDataSetInvalidated` here so that `ListView` reloads its rows after the number of conversations has been updated.

Last but not least, we need to modify the `OnLogin` method we set up earlier in `LoginActivity` to start our new activity as follows:

```
StartActivity(typeof(ConversationsActivity));
```

Now if we compile and run our application, we can navigate to a conversations list after logging in, as shown in the following screenshot:

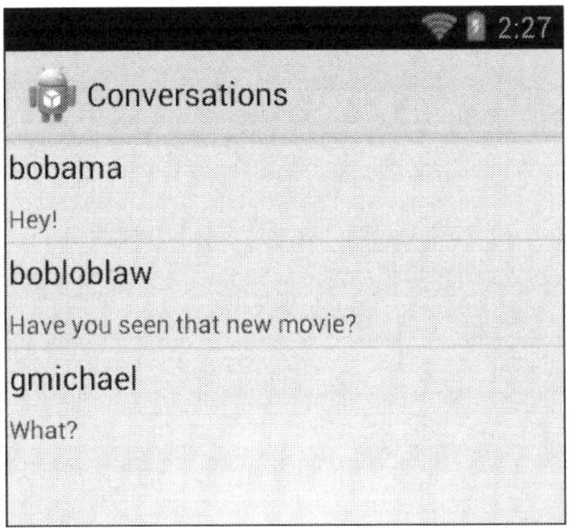

Implementing the friends list

Before we start implementing the friends list screen, we must first add a menu item to `ActionBar` in our application. Begin by creating a new `menu` folder within the `Resources` folder of our project. Next, create a new Android Layout file named `ConversationsMenu.axml`. Remove the default layout XML created and replace it with the following:

```xml
<?xml version="1.0" encoding="utf-8"?>
<menu xmlns:android="http://schemas.android.com/apk/res/android">
  <item android:id="@+id/addFriendMenu"
    android:icon="@android:drawable/ic_menu_add"
    android:showAsAction="ifRoom"/>
</menu>
```

We set up a root menu with one menu item inside it.

The following is a breakdown of what we set for the item in XML:

- `android:id`: We will use this later in C# to reference the menu item with `Resource.Id.addFriendMenu`.

- `android:icon`: This is an image resource to display the features for the menu item. We used a built-in Android one for a generic plus icon.

- `android:showAsAction`: This will make the menu item visible if there is room. If for some reason the device's screen is too narrow, an overflow menu will be displayed for the menu item.

Now we can make some changes in `ConversationsActivity.cs` to display the menu item as follows:

```
public override bool OnCreateOptionsMenu(IMenu menu)
{
  MenuInflater.Inflate(Resource.Menu.ConversationsMenu, menu);
  return base.OnCreateOptionsMenu(menu);
}
```

This code will take our layout and apply it to the menu at the top in our activity's action bar. Next, we can add some code to be run when the menu item is selected as follows:

```
public override bool OnOptionsItemSelected(IMenuItem item)
{
  if (item.ItemId == Resource.Id.addFriendMenu)
  {
    //TODO: launch the next activity
  }
  return base.OnOptionsItemSelected(item);
}
```

Now let's implement the next activity. Begin by making a copy of `Conversations.axml` found in the `layout` folder in the `Resources` directory and rename it to `Friends.axml`. The only change we'll make in this file will be to rename the ListView's ID to `@+id/friendsList`.

Next, perform the following steps to create a layout that can be used for the list items in `ListView`:

1. Make a new Android Layout called `FriendListItem.axml`.
2. Open the layout and switch to the **Source** tab found at the bottom of the screen.
3. Change the root `LinearLayout` XML element to a `RelativeLayout` element.
4. Switch back to the **Content** tab found at the bottom of the screen.
5. Drag a **Large Text** control from the **Toolbox** onto the layout and set **Id** to `@+id/friendName`.
6. Drag an **ImageView** control from the **Toolbox** onto the layout; you can either let **Id** be its default value or blank it out.

7. Change the image of `ImageView` to `@android:drawable/ic_menu_add`. This is the same plus icon we used earlier in the chapter. You can select it from the **Resources** dialog under the **Framework Resources** tab.

8. Set the **Width** and **Height** fields of both the controls to `wrap_content`. This is found under the **Layout** tab, under the **ViewGroup** section.

9. Next, check the value for **Align Parent Right** on just the image view.

10. Finally, set the **Margin** fields of both the controls to `3dp` in the **Layout** tab of the **Properties** box.

Using the Xamarin designer can be very productive, but some developers prefer a higher level of control. You might consider writing the XML code yourself as an alternative, which is fairly straightforward as in the following code:

```xml
<?xml version="1.0" encoding="utf-8"?>
<RelativeLayout
  xmlns:android="http://schemas.android.com/apk/res/android"
  android:layout_width="fill_parent"
  android:layout_height="fill_parent">
  <TextView
    android:text="Large Text"
    android:textAppearance="?android:attr/textAppearanceLarge"
    android:layout_width="wrap_content"
    android:layout_height="wrap_content"
    android:id="@+id/friendName"
    android:layout_margin="3dp" />
  <ImageView
    android:src="@android:drawable/ic_menu_add"
    android:layout_alignParentRight="true"
    android:layout_width="wrap_content"
    android:layout_height="wrap_content"
    android:layout_margin="3dp" />
</RelativeLayout>
```

Since we now have all the layouts we need for the new screen, let's create an Android Activity in the `Activities` folder named `FriendsActivity.cs`. Let's create the basic definition of the activity as follows, just like we did before:

```csharp
[Activity(Label = "Friends")]
public class FriendsActivity : BaseActivity<FriendViewModel>
{
  protected override void OnCreate(Bundle bundle)
  {
    base.OnCreate(bundle);
  }
}
```

Now, let's implement a nested `Adapter` class for setting up the list view items as follows:

```
class Adapter : BaseAdapter<User>
{
  readonly FriendViewModel friendViewModel =
    ServiceContainer.Resolve<FriendViewModel>();
  readonly LayoutInflater inflater;
  public Adapter(Context context)
  {
    inflater = (LayoutInflater)context.GetSystemService (
      Context.LayoutInflaterService);
  }
  public override long GetItemId(int position)
  {
    return friendViewModel.Friends [position].Id;
  }
  public override View GetView(
    int position, View convertView, ViewGroup parent)
  {
    if (convertView == null)
    {
      convertView = inflater.Inflate (
        Resource.Layout.FriendListItem, null);
    }
    var friend = this [position];
    var friendname = convertView.FindViewById<TextView>(
      Resource.Id.friendName);
    friendname.Text = friend.Username;
    return convertView;
  }
  public override int Count
  {
    get { return friendViewModel.Friends == null ? 0
      : friendViewModel.Friends.Length; }
  }
  public override User this[int index]
  {
    get { return friendViewModel.Friends [index]; }
  }
}.
```

There is really no difference in this adapter and the previous one we implemented for the conversations screen. We only have to set the friend's name, and we use the `User` object instead of the `Conversation` object.

To finish setting up the adapter, we can update the body of the `FriendsActivity` class as follows:

```
ListView listView;
Adapter adapter;
protected override void OnCreate(Bundle bundle)
{
  base.OnCreate(bundle);
  SetContentView(Resource.Layout.Friends);
  listView = FindViewById<ListView>(Resource.Id.friendsList);
  listView.Adapter =
    adapter = new Adapter(this);
}
protected async override void OnResume()
{
  base.OnResume();
  try
  {
    await viewModel.GetFriends();
    adapter.NotifyDataSetInvalidated();
  }
  catch (Exception exc)
  {
    DisplayError(exc);
  }
}
```

And last but not least, we can update `OnOptionsItemSelected` in the `ConversationsActivity` class as follows:

```
public override bool OnOptionsItemSelected(IMenuItem item)
{
  if (item.ItemId == Resource.Id.addFriendMenu)
  {
    StartActivity(typeof(FriendsActivity));
  }
  return base.OnOptionsItemSelected(item);
}
```

So if we compile and run the application, we can navigate to a fully implemented friends list screen, as shown in the following screenshot:

Composing messages

The next screen is a bit more complicated; we will need to create a ListView that uses multiple layout files for each row, depending on the type of the row. We'll also need to perform some layout tricks to place a view below the ListView and set up ListView to autoscroll.

For the next screen, let's begin by creating a new layout named Messages.axml in the layout folder of the Resources directory and then perform the following steps:

1. Drag a new **ListView** onto the layout. Set **Id** to @+id/messageList.

2. Check the box for **Stack From Bottom** and set **Transcript Mode** to alwaysScroll. This will set it up to display items from the bottom up.

3. Set the **Weight** value to 1 for **ListView** in the **Layout** tab under the **LinearLayout** section.

4. Drag a new **RelativeLayout** control onto the layout. Let **Id** be the default value, or remove it.

5. Drag a new **Button** control inside **RelativeLayout**. Set **Id** to @+id/sendButton.

6. Check the box for **Align Parent Right** in the **Layout** tab.

7. Drag a new **Plain Text** control found in the **Text Field** section inside **RelativeLayout** to the left of the button. Set **Id** to @+id/messageText.

8. In the **Layout** tab, set **To Left Of** to @+id/sendButton, and set **Width** to match_parent.

9. Check the box for **Center in Parent** to fix the vertical centering..

When completed, the XML file will be as follows:

```xml
<?xml version="1.0" encoding="utf-8"?>
<LinearLayout
  xmlns:android="http://schemas.android.com/apk/res/android"
  android:orientation="vertical"
  android:layout_width="match_parent"
  android:layout_height="match_parent">
  <ListView
    android:minWidth="25px"
    android:minHeight="25px"
    android:layout_width="fill_parent"
    android:layout_height="wrap_content"
    android:id="@+id/messageList"
    android:layout_weight="1"
    android:stackFromBottom="true"
    android:transcriptMode="alwaysScroll" />
  <RelativeLayout
    android:minWidth="25px"
    android:minHeight="25px"
    android:layout_width="fill_parent"
    android:layout_height="wrap_content">
  <Button
    android:text="Send"
    android:layout_alignParentRight="true"
    android:layout_width="wrap_content"
    android:layout_height="wrap_content"
    android:id="@+id/sendButton" />
  <EditText
    android:layout_width="match_parent"
    android:layout_height="wrap_content"
    android:layout_toLeftOf="@id/sendButton"
    android:layout_centerInParent="true"
    android:id="@+id/messageText" />
  </RelativeLayout>
</LinearLayout>
```

Next, perform the following steps to make two more Android layouts:

1. Create a new layout named `MyMessageListItem.axml` in the `layout` folder of the `Resources` directory.

2. Open the layout and switch to the **Source** tab. Change the root XML element to a `RelativeLayout`.

3. Switch back to the **Content** tab and drag two **TextView** controls onto the layout.

4. In the **Id** field, enter `@+id/myMessageText` and `@+id/myMessageDate` respectively.

5. For both the views, set **Margin** to `3dp`, and **Width** and **Height** to `wrap_content`.

6. For the first TextView, set **Color** under the **Style** tab to `@android:color/ holo_blue_bright`.

7. For the second TextView, check the **Align Parent Right** checkbox under the **Layout** tab.

8. Create a new layout named `TheirMessageListItem.axml` and repeat the process. Select a different color for the first TextView in the new layout.

Finally, we'll need to create a new activity for the screen. Create a new Android Activity named `MessagesActivity.cs` in the `Activities` directory. Begin with the standard code to set up an activity as follows:

```
[Activity(Label = "Messages")]
public class MessagesActivity : BaseActivity<MessageViewModel>
{
  protected override void OnCreate(Bundle bundle)
  {
    base.OnCreate(bundle);
  }
}
```

Next, let's implement a more complicated adapter than we implemented earlier, as follows:

```
class Adapter : BaseAdapter<Message>
{
  readonly MessageViewModel messageViewModel =
    ServiceContainer.Resolve<MessageViewModel>();
  readonly ISettings settings =
    ServiceContainer.Resolve<ISettings>();
  readonly LayoutInflater inflater;
  const int MyMessageType = 0, TheirMessageType = 1;
  public Adapter (Context context)
  {
    inflater = (LayoutInflater)context.GetSystemService (
      Context.LayoutInflaterService);
  }
  public override long GetItemId(int position)
  {
    return messageViewModel.Messages [position].Id;
  }
```

```
public override int Count
{
  get { return messageViewModel.Messages == null ? 0
    : messageViewModel.Messages.Length; }
}
public override Message this[int index]
{
  get { return messageViewModel.Messages [index]; }
}
public override int ViewTypeCount
{
  get { return 2; }
}
public override int GetItemViewType(int position)
{
  var message = this [position];
  return message.UserId == settings.User.Id ?
    MyMessageType : TheirMessageType;
}
}
```

This includes everything except our implementation of GetView, which we'll get to shortly. The first changes here are some constants for MyMessageType and TheirMessageType. We then implemented ViewTypeCount and GetItemViewType. This is Android's mechanism for using two different layouts for list items in a list view. We use one type of layout for the user's messages and a different one for the other user in the conversation.

Next, let's implement GetView as follows:

```
public override View GetView(
  int position, View convertView, ViewGroup parent)
{
  var message = this [position];
  int type = GetItemViewType(position);
  if (convertView == null)
  {
    if (type == MyMessageType)
    {
      convertView = inflater.Inflate(
        Resource.Layout.MyMessageListItem, null);
    }
    else
    {
      convertView = inflater.Inflate(
        Resource.Layout.TheirMessageListItem, null);
```

```
      }
    }
    TextView messageText, dateText;
    if (type == MyMessageType)
    {
      messageText = convertView.FindViewById<TextView>(
        Resource.Id.myMessageText);
      dateText = convertView.FindViewById<TextView>(
        Resource.Id.myMessageDate);
    }
    else
    {
      messageText = convertView.FindViewById<TextView>(
        Resource.Id.theirMessageText);
      dateText = convertView.FindViewById<TextView>(
        Resource.Id.theirMessageDate);
      }
    messageText.Text = message.Text;
    dateText.Text = message.Date.ToString("MM/dd/yy HH:mm");
    return convertView;
}
```

Let's break down our implementation through the following steps:

1. We first pull out the `message` object for the position of the row.

2. Next, we grab the view type that determines whether it is the current user's message or the other user in the conversation.

3. If `convertView` is `null`, we inflate the appropriate layout based on the type.

4. Next, we pull the two text views, `messageText` and `dateText`, out of `convertView`. We have to use the type value to make sure we use the correct resource IDs.

5. We set the appropriate text on both text views using the `message` object.

6. We return `convertView`.

Now let's finish `MessagesActivity` by setting up the rest of the adapter. First, let's implement some member variables and the `OnCreate` method as follows:

```
ListView listView;
EditText messageText;
Button sendButton;
Adapter adapter;
protected override void OnCreate(Bundle bundle)
{
  base.OnCreate(bundle);
  Title = viewModel.Conversation.Username;
```

```
SetContentView(Resource.Layout.Messages);
listView = FindViewById<ListView>(Resource.Id.messageList);
messageText = FindViewById<EditText>(Resource.Id.messageText);
sendButton = FindViewById<Button>(Resource.Id.sendButton);
listView.Adapter =
  adapter = new Adapter(this);
sendButton.Click += async (sender, e) =>
{
  viewModel.Text = messageText.Text;
  try
  {
    await viewModel.SendMessage();
    messageText.Text = string.Empty;
    adapter.NotifyDataSetInvalidated();
    listView.SetSelection(adapter.Count);
  }
  catch (Exception exc)
  {
    DisplayError(exc);
  }
};
}
```

So far, this activity is fairly standard compared to our previous activities in this chapter. We also had to wire up the `Click` event of `sendButton` in `OnCreate` so that it sends the message and refreshes the list. We also used a trick to scroll the list view to the end by setting its selection to the last item.

Next, we'll need to implement `OnResume` to load the messages, invalidate the adapter, and then scroll the list view to the end, as follows:

```
protected async override void OnResume()
{
  base.OnResume();
  try
  {
    await viewModel.GetMessages();
    adapter.NotifyDataSetInvalidated();
    listView.SetSelection(adapter.Count);
  }
  catch (Exception exc)
  {
    DisplayError(exc);
  }
}
```

So finally, if you compile and run the app, you will be able to navigate to the messages screen and add new messages to the list, as shown in the following screenshot:

Summary

In this chapter, we started by going over the basic settings in the Android Manifest file. Next, we implemented a custom `Application` class for setting up our `ServiceContainer`. We then went over the different types of Android layouts and implemented a login screen using native Android views. Next, we set up a menu in the Android action bar by using an Android layout and overriding a few built-in methods. We implemented the friends list screen, and learned the basics of `ListView` and adapters. Finally, we implemented the messages screen, and used the more advanced functionality available in list view adapters and layouts.

Upon completing this chapter, you will have a partially functional Android version of XamChat. You will have gained a deeper understanding of the Android SDK and tools. You should be confident on developing your own Android applications using Xamarin. Take it upon yourself to implement the remaining screens that we did not cover in the chapter. If you get lost, feel free to review the full sample application included with this book. In the next chapter, we'll cover how to deploy to mobile devices and why is it very important to test your applications on real devices.

7
Deploying and Testing on Devices

Deploying to devices is both important and a bit of a hassle when you try it the first time. Testing on a device will commonly display performance issues that aren't present in the simulator/emulator of your application. You can also test things that are only possible on real devices such as GPS, camera, memory limitations, or cellular network connectivity. There are also common pitfalls that exist when developing for Xamarin, which will only surface when testing on a real device.

In this chapter, we will cover:

- iOS provisioning
- Android device settings for debugging
- The linker
- Ahead of time (AOT) compilation
- Common memory pitfalls with Xamarin

Before we begin this chapter, it is important to note that an iOS Developer Program membership is required to deploy to iOS devices. Feel free to go back to *Chapter 1, Xamarin Setup* to walk through that process.

iOS provisioning

Apple has a strict process for deploying applications to iOS devices. While being quite convoluted and sometimes painful for developers, Apple can enable a certain level of security by preventing the average user from sideloading potentially malicious applications.

Before we can deploy our application to an iOS device, there are a few things we will need to set up in the **iOS Dev Center**. We will begin by creating an App ID or bundle ID for your account. This is the primary identifier for any iOS application.

Begin by navigating to `http://developer.apple.com` and perform the following steps:

1. Click on the **iOS Dev Center** link.
2. Sign in with your developer account.
3. Click on **Certificates, Identifiers, & Profiles** on the right-hand side navigation.
4. Click on **Identifiers**.
5. Click on the plus button to add a new Apple ID.
6. In the **Name** field, enter something meaningful such as `YourCompanyWildcard`.
7. Select the **Wildcard App ID** radio button.
8. In the **Bundle ID** field, select a reverse domain styled name for your company such as `com.yourcompanyname.*`.
9. Click on **Continue**.
10. Review the final setting and hit **Submit**.

Leave this web page open as we will be using it throughout the chapter.

We just registered a wildcard bundle ID for your account; use this as a prefix for all future applications you wish to identify with this account. Later, when you are preparing to deploy an app to the Apple App Store, you will create an **Explicit App ID** such as `com.yourcompany.yourapp`. This allows you to deploy the specific app to the store, while the wildcard ID is best used for deploying to devices for testing.

Next we need to locate the unique identifier on each device you plan to debug your application on. Apple requires each device to be registered under your account with a limit of 200 devices per developer. The only way to circumvent this requirement is to register for the iOS Developer Enterprise program with a $299 yearly fee, which does not include the standard $99 developer fee.

Begin by launching Xcode and perform the following steps:

1. Click on **Window** | **Organizer** in the menu.
2. Make sure the **Devices** tab is selected.
3. Plug in your target device with a USB cable.
4. On the left-hand side navigation, you should see your device's name; select it.
5. Notice the **Identifier** value for your device. Copy it to your clipboard.

The following screenshot shows what your screen should look like with your device selected in Xcode:

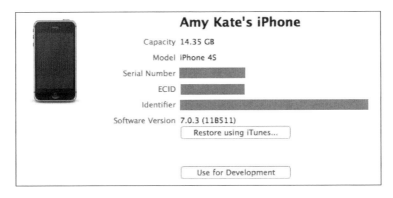

Return to http://developer.apple.com (hopefully, it is still open from earlier in the chapter) and perform the following steps:

1. Click on **Devices** on the left-hand side navigation.
2. Click on the plus button in the top-right corner of the dialog.
3. Enter a meaningful name for your device and paste the **Identifier** from your clipboard into the **UDID** field.
4. Click on **Continue**.
5. Review the information you entered and hit **Register**.

Down the road, when your account is fully set up, you can just click on the **Use for Development** button in Xcode and skip this second set of steps.

The following screenshot shows what your device list should look like when complete:

Next, we will need to generate a certificate to represent you as the developer for your account. Prior to Xcode 5, you had to create a certificate signing request by using the **Keychain** app on your Mac. Xcode 5 makes things a lot easier by integrating a lot of this process into Xcode.

Open Xcode and perform the following steps:

1. Navigate to **Xcode** | **Preferences** in the menu at the top.

2. Select the **Accounts** tab.

3. Click on the plus button on the bottom left and then click on **Add Apple ID**.

4. Enter your e-mail address and password for your developer account.

5. Upon creating the account, click on **View Details** on the bottom right.

6. Click on the sync button on the bottom left.

7. If this is a new account, Xcode will display a warning that no certificates exist yet. Check each box and click on **Request** to generate the certificates.

Xcode will now automatically create a developer certificate for your account and install it into your Mac's keychain.

The following screenshot shows what your screen will look like during the process:

Next, we need to create a **provisioning profile**. This is the final file that allows applications to be installed on an iOS device. A provisioning profile contains an App ID, a list of devices IDs, and finally, a certificate for the developer. You must also have the private key of the developer certificate in your Mac's keychain to use a provisioning profile.

The following are a few types of provisioning profiles:

- **Development**: This is used for debugging or release builds; you will actively use this type of profile when your applications are in development.
- **Ad Hoc**: This is used mainly for release builds; this type of certificate is great for beta testing or distribution to a small set of users. You can distribute to an unlimited number of users using this method with an enterprise developer account.
- **App Store**: This is used for release builds for submission to the App Store. You cannot deploy an app to your device using this certificate; it can only be used for store submission.

Let's return to `http://developer.apple.com` and create a new provisioning profile by performing the following steps:

1. Click on **Provisioning Profiles** on the left-hand side navigation.
2. Click on the plus button on the top-right corner of the dialog.
3. Select **iOS App Development** and click on **Continue**.
4. Select your wildcard App ID created earlier in the chapter and click on **Continue**.
5. Select the certificate we created earlier in the chapter and click on **Continue**.
6. Select the devices you want to deploy to and click on **Continue**.
7. Enter an appropriate **Profile Name** such as `YourCompanyDev`.
8. Click on **Generate** and your provisioning profile will be created.

The following screenshot shows the new profile that you will end up with upon creation. Don't worry about downloading the file; we'll use Xcode to import the final profile.

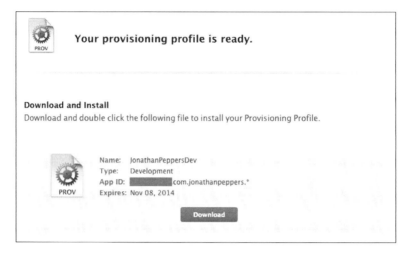

To import the provisioning profile, return to Xcode and perform the following steps:

1. Navigate to **Xcode** | **Preferences** in the menu at the top of the dialog.
2. Select the **Accounts** tab.
3. Select your account and click on **View Details**.
4. Click on the sync button on the bottom left.
5. After a few seconds, your provisioning profiles will appear.

The following screenshot shows what your preferences in Xcode should look like; although you may not have as many profiles as this yet. Xcode will also create a few profiles on its own.

In the latest version of Xamarin Studio, you can view these profiles but will not be able to sync them. Navigate to **Xamarin Studio** | **Preferences** | **Developer Accounts** to view the provisioning profiles from Xamarin Studio. You can also see Xamarin's documentation on iOS provisioning on their documentation website at `http://docs.xamarin.com/guides/ios/getting_started/device_provisioning/`.

lroid device settings

ıred to the hassle of deploying your application on iOS devices, Android is a
:. To deploy an application to a device, you merely have to set a few settings
! device. This is due to Android's openness in comparison to iOS. Android
‥ e debugging is turned off for most users, but it can be easily turned on by any
developer that may wish to take a try at writing Android applications.

Begin by opening the **Settings** application. You may have to locate this by looking
through all the applications on the device as follows:

1. Scroll down and click on the section labeled **Developer options**.
2. In the action bar at the top, you may have to toggle a switch to the **ON** position. This varies on each device.
3. Scroll down and check **USB Debugging**.
4. A warning confirmation will appear; click on **OK**.

> Note that some newer Android devices have made it a little more
> difficult for the average user to turn on USB debugging. You have to
> click on the **Developer options** item seven times to turn this option
> on. Google must have felt that the settings menu to turn on developer
> options was too boring.

The following screenshot shows what your device will look like during the process:

After enabling this option, all you have to do is plug in your device via USB and debug an Android application in Xamarin Studio. You will see your device listed in the **Select Device** dialog. Note that if you are on Windows or have a non standard device, you may have to visit your device vendor's website to install the drivers. Most Samsung and Nexus devices install their drivers automatically. On Android 4.3 and higher, there is also a confirmation dialog on the device that appears before beginning a USB debugging session.

The following screenshot shows what your device will look like for a Samsung Galaxy SII in the **Select Device** dialog. Xamarin Studio will display the model number, which is not always a name that you may recognize. You can view this model number in your device's settings.

Understanding the linker

To keep Xamarin applications small and lightweight for mobile devices, Xamarin has created a feature for their compiler called the **linker**. Its main purpose is to strip unused code out of the core Mono assemblies (such as `System.dll`) and platform-specific assemblies (`Mono.Android.dll` and `monotouch.dll`); however, it can also give you the same benefits if set up to run on your own assemblies. Without running the linker, the entire Mono framework can be around 30 megabytes. This is why linking is enabled by default in device builds, which enables you to keep your applications small.

The linker uses static analysis to work through the various code paths in an assembly. If it determines a method or class that is never used, it removes the unused code from that assembly. This can be a time-consuming process, so builds running in the simulator skip this step by default.

Xamarin applications have the following three main settings for the linker:

- **Don't Link**: With this option, the linker compilation step is skipped. This is best for builds running in the simulator or if you need to diagnose a potential issue with the linker.

- **Link SDK Assemblies Only**: With this option, the linker will only be run on the core Mono assemblies such as System.dll, System.Core.dll, and System.Xml.dll.

- **Link All Assemblies**: With this option, the linker is run against all the assemblies in your application, which include any class libraries or third party assemblies you are using.

These settings can be found in the **Project** options of any Xamarin.iOS or Xamarin. Android application. These settings are generally not present in class libraries as it is generally associated with an iOS or Android application that will be deployed.

The linker can also cause potential issues as there are cases in which its analysis determines incorrectly that a piece of code is unused. This can happen if you are using classes in the System.Reflection namespace instead of accessing the method or property directly. This is one reason why it is important for you to test your application on physical devices, as linking is enabled for device builds.

To demonstrate this issue, let's look at the following code example:

```
//Just a simple class for holding info
public class Person
{
  public int Id { get; set; }
  public string Name { get; set; }
}

//Then somewhere later in your code
var person = new Person { Id = 1, Name = "Chuck Norris" };
var propInfo = person.GetType().GetProperty("Name");
string value = propInfo.GetValue(person) as string;
Console.WriteLine("Name: " + value);
```

Running the preceding code will work fine using the options for **Don't Link** or **Link SDK Assemblies Only**. However, if you try to run this when using **Link All Assemblies**, you will get an exception similar to the following:

```
Unhandled Exception:
System.ArgumentException: Get Method not found for 'Name'
   at System.Reflection.MonoProperty.GetValue (System.Object obj,
   BindingFlags invokeAttr, System.Reflection.Binder binder,
   System.Object[] index, System.Globalization.CultureInfo culture)
   at System.Reflection.PropertyInfo.GetValue (System.Object obj)
```

Since the Name property's getter was never used directly from code, the linker stripped it from the assembly. This caused the reflection code to fail at runtime.

Even though potential issues can arise in your code, the option of **Link All Assemblies** is still quite useful. There are a few optimizations that can only be performed in this mode, and Xamarin can reduce your application to the smallest possible size. If performance or a tiny download size is the requirement for your application, give this option a try. However, thorough testing should be performed to verify that no problems are caused by linking your assemblies.

To resolve issues in your code, Xamarin has included a complete set of workarounds to prevent specific parts of your code from being stripped away.

Some of the options include:

- Mark class members with [Preserve]: This will force the linker to include the attributed method, field, or property.

- Mark an entire class with [Preserve(AllMembers=true)]: This will preserve all code within the class.

- Mark an entire assembly with [assembly: Preserve]: This is an assembly-level attribute that will preserve all code contained within it.

- Skip an entire assembly by modifying **Additional mtouch arguments** in your project options: Use --linkskip=System to skip an entire assembly. This can be used on assemblies that you do not have the source code for.

- Custom linking via an XML file: This is the best option when you need to skip linking on a specific class or method that you do not have the source code for. Use --xml=YourFile.xml in **Additional mtouch arguments**.

The following is a sample XML file that demonstrates custom linking:

```xml
<linker>
  <assembly fullname="mscorlib">
    <type fullname="System.Environment">
      <field name="mono_corlib_version" />
        <method name="get_StackTrace" />
    </type>
  </assembly>
  <assembly fullname="My.Assembly.Name">
    <type fullname="MyTypeA" preserve="fields" />
      <method name=".ctor" />
    </type>
    <type fullname="MyTypeB" />
      <method signature="System.Void MyFunc(System.Int32 x)" />
        <field signature="System.String _myField" />
    </type>
  </assembly>
</linker>
```

Custom linking is the most complicated option and is usually the last resort. Luckily, most Xamarin applications will not have to work around many linker issues.

Understanding AOT compilation

The runtime behind Mono and .NET on Windows is based on a **just in time (JIT)** compiler. C# and other .NET languages are compiled into **Microsoft intermediate language (MSIL)**. At runtime, MSIL is compiled into a native code to run on whatever type of architecture is running your application. Xamarin.Android follows this exact pattern. However, due to Apple's restrictions on dynamically generated code, a JIT compiler is not allowed on iOS.

To work around this restriction, Xamarin has developed a new option called **ahead of time (AOT)** compilation. In addition to making .NET possible on iOS, AOT has other benefits such as a shorter startup time and potentially better performance.

AOT also has some limitations that are generally related to C# generics. To compile an assembly ahead of time, the compiler will need to run some static analysis against your code to determine type information. Generics throw a wrench into this situation.

There are a few cases that are not supported with AOT, but are completely valid in C#. The first is a generic interface as follows:

```
interface MyInterface<T>
{
   T GetMyValue();
}
```

The compiler cannot determine the classes that may implement this interface ahead of time, especially when multiple assemblies are involved. The second limitation is related to the first. You cannot override virtual methods that contain generic parameters or return values.

The following is a simple example:

```
class MyClass<T>
{
   public virtual T GetMyValue()
   {
      //Some code here
   }
}

class MySubClass : MyClass<int>
{
   public override int GetMyValue()
   {
      //Some code here
   }
}
```

Again, the static analysis of the compiler cannot determine which classes may override this method at compile time.

Another limitation is the inability to create a generic class that derives from NSObject as follows:

```
class MyGenericObject<T> : UIView
{
   //Code here
}
```

Since NSObject is a native object on iOS, it is currently not compatible with C# generics.

Lastly, you cannot use `DllImport` in a generic class as shown in the following code:

```
class MyGeneric<T>
{
  [DllImport("MyImport")]
  public static void MyImport();
}
```

If you are not familiar with the language feature, `DllImport` is a way to call native C/C++ methods from C#. Using them inside generic classes is not supported.

These limitations are another good reason why testing on devices is important, since the preceding code will work fine on other platforms that can run C# code but not Xamarin.iOS.

Avoiding common memory pitfalls

Memory on mobile devices is certainly not an unlimited commodity. Because of this, memory usage in your application can be much more important than on desktop applications. At times, you might find the need to use a memory profiler, or improve your code to use memory more efficiently.

The following are the most common memory pitfalls:

- The **garbage collector (GC)** is unable to collect large objects fast enough to keep up with your application
- Your code inadvertently causes a memory leak
- A C# object is garbage collected but is later attempted to be used by native code.

Let's take a look at the first problem where the GC cannot keep up. Let's say, we have a Xamarin.iOS application with a button for sharing an image on Twitter as follows:

```
twitterShare.TouchUpInside += (sender, e) =>
{
  var image = UIImage.FromFile("YourLargeImage.png");
  //Share to Twitter
};
```

Now let's assume the image is a 10 MB image from the user's camera roll. If the user clicks on the button and cancels the Twitter post rapidly, there could be the possibility of your application running out of memory. iOS will commonly force close apps using too much memory, and you don't want users to experience this with your app.

The best solution is to call `Dispose` on the image when you are finished with it as follows:

```
var image = UIImage.FromFile("YourLargeImage.png");
//Share to Twitter
image.Dispose();
```

An even better approach would be to take advantage of the C# `using` statement as follows:

```
using(var image = UIImage.FromFile("YourLargeImage.png"))
{
    //Share to Twitter
}
```

The C# `using` statement will automatically call `Dispose` in a `try-finally` block, so the object will get disposed even if an exception is thrown. I recommend taking advantage of the `using` statement for any `IDisposable` class where possible. It is not always necessary for small objects such as `NSString`, but is always a good idea for larger, more heavyweight `UIKit` objects.

 A similar situation can occur on Android with the `Bitmap` class. Although slightly different, it is best to call both the `Dispose` and `Recycle` methods on this class along with using the `BitmapFactory`. `Options` settings for `InPurgeable` and `InInputShareable`.

Memory leaks are the next potential issues. C# being a managed, garbage-collected language prevents a lot of memory leaks, but not all of them. The most common leaks in C# are caused by events.

Let's assume we have a static class with an event as follows:

```
static class MyStatic
{
    public static event EventHandler MyEvent;
}
```

Now, let's say we need to subscribe to the event from an iOS controller as follows:

```
public override void ViewDidLoad()
{
    base.ViewDidLoad();

    MyStatic.MyEvent += (sender, e) =>
    {
        //Do something
    };
}
```

The problem here is that the static class will hold a reference to the controller until the event is unsubscribed. This is a situation that a lot of developers might miss. To fix this issue on iOS, I would subscribe to the event in `ViewWillAppear` and unsubscribe `ViewWillDisappear`. On Android, use `OnStart` and `OnStop`, or `OnPause` and `OnResume`.

You would correctly implement this event as follows:

```
public override void ViewWillAppear()
{
  base.ViewWillAppear();
  MyStatic.MyEvent += OnMyEvent;
}

public override void ViewWillDisappear()
{
  base.ViewWillDisappear ();
  MyStatic.MyEvent += OnMyEvent;
}
```

However, an event is not a surefire cause of a memory leak. Subscribing to the `TouchUpInside` event on a button inside the `ViewDidLoad` method, for example, is just fine. Since the button lives in memory just as long as the controller, everything can get garbage collected without problem.

For the final issue, the garbage collector can sometimes remove a C# object; later, an Objective-C object attempts to access it.

The following is an example of adding a button to `UITableViewCell`:

```
public override UITableViewCell GetCell(
  UITableView tableView, NSIndexPath indexPath)
{
  var cell = tableView.DequeueReusableCell("MyCell");
  //Remaining cell setup here

  var button = UIButton.FromType(UIButtonType.InfoDark);
  button.TouchUpInside += (sender, e) =>
  {
    //Do something
  };
  cell.AccessoryView = button;
  return cell;
}
```

We add the built-in info button as an accessory view to the cell. The problem here is that the button will get garbage collected, but its Objective-C counterpart will remain in use as it is displayed on the screen. If you click on the button after a period of time, you will get a crash that looks something like the following:

```
mono-rt: Stacktrace:

mono-rt:    at <unknown>

mono-rt:    at (wrapper managed-to-native) MonoTouch.UIKit.UIApplication.
UIApplicationMain (int,string[],intptr,intptr)

mono-rt:    at MonoTouch.UIKit.UIApplication.Main (string[],string,string)

... Continued ...

==================================================================

Got a SIGSEGV while executing native code. This usually indicates

a fatal error in the mono runtime or one of the native libraries

used by your application.

==================================================================
```

It is not the most descriptive error message, but in general, you know that something went wrong in the native Objective-C code. To resolve the issue, create a custom subclass of `UITableViewCell` and create a dedicated member variable for the button as follows:

```
public class MyCell : UITableViewCell
{
  UIButton button;
  public MyCell()
  {
    button = UIButton.FromType(UIButtonType.InfoDark);
    button.TouchUpInside += (sender, e) =>
    {
      //Do something
    };
    AccessoryView = button;
  }
}
```

Now, your `GetCell` implementation will look something like the following:

```
public override UITableViewCell GetCell(
  UITableView tableView, NSIndexPath indexPath)
{
  var cell = tableView.DequeueReusableCell("MyCell") as MyCell;
  //Remaining cell setup here

  return cell;
}
```

Since the button is not a local variable, it will no longer get garbage collected very soon. A crash is avoided, and in some ways this code is a bit cleaner. Similar situations can happen on Android with the interaction between C# and Java; however, it is less likely since both are garbage-collected languages.

Summary

In this chapter, we started out learning the process of setting up iOS provision profiles to deploy to iOS devices. Next, we looked at the required device settings to deploy your application to an Android device. We discovered the Xamarin linker and how it can make your applications smaller and perform better. We went over the various settings to resolve problems caused by your code and the linker, and we explained AOT compilation on iOS and the limitations that occur. Finally, we covered the most common memory pitfalls that can occur with Xamarin applications.

Testing your Xamarin application on mobile devices is important for various reasons. Some bugs are only displayed on the device due to the platform limitations that Xamarin has to work around. Your PC is much more powerful, so you will see different performance using the simulator rather than on a physical device. In the next chapter, we'll create a real web service using Windows Azure to drive our XamChat application. We will use a feature called Azure Mobile Services and implement push notifications on iOS and Android.

8
Web Services with Push Notifications

Modern mobile applications are defined by their network connectivity. A mobile app that does not interact with a web server is both a rare find and potentially a boring application. In this book, we'll use the **Windows Azure** cloud platform to implement a server-side backend for our XamChat application. We'll use a feature called **Azure Mobile Services**, which is an excellent fit for our application and has the benefit of built-in push notifications. Once we are done with this chapter, our XamChat sample application will be much closer to being a real application and will allow its users to interact with one another.

In this chapter, we will cover:

- The services offered by Windows Azure
- Setting up your Azure account
- Azure Mobile Services as a backend for XamChat
- Creating tables and scripts
- Implementing a real web service for XamChat
- Using the Apple Push Notification service
- Sending notifications with Google Cloud Messaging

Learning Windows Azure

Windows Azure is an excellent cloud platform released by Microsoft in 2010. Azure provides both **Infrastructure as a Service (IaaS)** and **Platform as a Service (PaaS)** for building modern web applications and services. This means that it provides you with access to direct virtual machines within which you can deploy any operating system or software of your choice. This is known as IaaS. Azure also provides multiple platforms for building applications such as **Azure websites** or **SQL Azure**. These platforms are known as PaaS, since you deploy your software at a high level and do not have to deal directly with virtual machines or manage software upgrades.

Let's go over the following more commonly used services provided by Windows Azure:

- **Virtual Machines**: Azure provides you with access to virtual machines of all sizes. You can install practically any operating system of your choice; there are many premade distributions to choose from within Azure's gallery.

- **Websites**: You can deploy any type of website that will run in Microsoft IIS from ASP .NET sites to **PHP** or **Node.js**.

- **SQL Azure**: This is a cloud-based version of Microsoft SQL Server, which is a fully featured **RDMS (Relational Database Management System)** for storing data.

- **Mobile services**: This is a simple platform for building web services for mobile apps. It uses **SQL Azure** for backend storage and a simple JavaScript scripting system based on Node.js for adding business logic.

- **Storage**: Azure provides **blob storage**, a method for storing binary files and **table storage**, which is a **NoSQL** solution for persisting data.

- **Service bus**: This is a cloud-based solution for creating queues to facilitate communication between other cloud services. It also includes notification hubs as a simple way for providing push notifications to mobile apps.

- **Worker roles**: A simple way to run a custom process in the cloud can be a plain Windows executable or a .NET worker role project.

- **Cloud services**: This is a conglomeration of other services. Cloud services allow you to bundle multiple services together and create staging and production environments. It is a great tool for deployment; you can deploy changes to staging and swap staging and production to preserve uptime for your users.

Apart from these services, there are many more and new ones are added pretty regularly. We will use **Azure Mobile Services**, which leverages SQL Azure, to build our web service for XamChat. You can visit `http://windowsazure.com` for a full rundown of pricing and services offered.

In this book, we chose to demonstrate a solution using Windows Azure as a backend for XamChat, since it is very easy to use with Xamarin applications due to the fantastic library in the Xamarin Component Store. However, there are many more choices out there besides Azure, which you may want to consider. Xamarin does not limit the types of web services your applications can interact with.

Here are a few service providers commonly used for mobile applications:

- **Parse**: This service provides a product similar to that of Azure Mobile Services, complete with data storage and push notifications. You can get more information at `http://parse.com`.

- **Urban airship**: This service provides push notifications for mobile apps across multiple platforms. You can get more information at `http://urbanairship.com`.

- **Amazon web services**: This service is a complete cloud solution that is equivalent to Windows Azure. It has everything you need to deploy applications in the cloud with total virtual machine support. You can get more information at `http://aws.amazon.com`.

Additionally, you can develop your own web services with on-premises web servers or inexpensive hosting services using the languages and technologies of your choice.

Setting up your Azure account

To start developing with Windows Azure, you can subscribe to a free one month trial along with free credit worth $200. To go along with this, many of its services have free tiers that give you lower performance versions. So if your trial expires, you can continue your development at little or no cost, depending on the services you are using.

Begin by navigating to `http://windowsazure.com/pricing/free-trial` and carry out the following steps:

1. Click on the **Try it now** link.
2. Sign in with a Windows Live ID.
3. For security purposes, verify your account via your phone or a text message.
4. Enter the payment information. This is only used if you exceed your spending limits. You won't accidentally spend beyond budget by developing your app — you will only spend money once a couple hundred users are interacting with your services.
5. Check **I agree** to the policies and click on **Sign Up**.
6. Review the final setting and click on **Submit**.

If all the required information is entered correctly, you will now have access to the Azure subscription page. Your subscription page will look like the following screenshot:

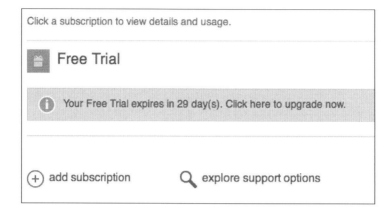

You can click the **Portal** link in the top-right corner of the page to access your account. In the future, you can manage your Azure services at `http://manage.windowsazure.com`.

Complete the Windows Azure Tour to get a quick rundown of the management portal's features. You can then access the main menu to create new Azure services, virtual machines, and so on. The main menu looks like the following screenshot:

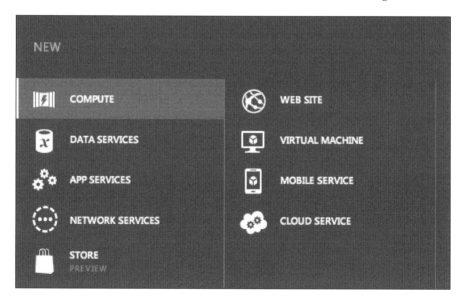

This concludes your sign up for Windows Azure. It is pretty simple compared to the Apple and Google Play developer programs. Feel free to play around and keep in mind that it is difficult to spend money accidentally unless you are delivering content to real users. Azure has free versions of most services and also delivers a good amount of bandwidth for free. You can get more information on pricing at `http://windowsazure.com/en-us/pricing/overview`.

Note that there are a lot of misconceptions about Windows Azure being expensive. You can do all of your development for an application on the free tier without spending a dime. When putting applications into production, you can easily scale up or down on the number of VM instances to keep your costs under control. In general, you will not be spending a lot of money if you do not have a lot of users, and luckily you should be making plenty of money if you have lots of users.

Exploring Azure Mobile Services

For the server side of XamChat, we'll use Azure Mobile Services to provide backend storage to the application. Azure Mobile Service is a neat solution to accelerate development for mobile applications that provide data storage and a **REST-based** API. It also includes a .NET client library for interacting with the service from C#.

A few nice features of Azure Mobile Services are as follows:

- Storage of data in the cloud with SQL Azure, or other Azure data services such as blob or table storage
- Easy authentication with Windows Live ID, Facebook, Google, or Twitter
- Push notifications with iOS, Android, and Windows devices
- An easy-to-use .NET library for client-side development
- Scale Azure Mobile Services to accommodate high volumes of data

You can see why using Azure Mobile Services is a good choice for simple mobile applications. The benefits of accelerated development and the many features it provides are a great fit for our XamChat sample application.

Navigate to your account at `http://manage.windowsazure.com` and perform the following steps to create a Mobile Service:

1. Click on the plus button in the bottom-left of the window.
2. Navigate to **Compute** | **Mobile Service** | **Create** through the menu.
3. Enter a domain URL of your choice such as `yourname-xamchat`.
4. We use the free database option for now.
5. Select a data center near your location in the **Region** dropdown.

6. Now, click on **Next**.

7. Use the default database name, and choose **New SQL database server**.

8. Enter a login name and password for the SQL server and keep this information in a safe place.

9. Make sure the region is the same as that of your mobile service to ensure performance.

10. Review your final settings and hit the **Finish** button.

The management portal will display progress, and it could take several seconds to create your mobile service and SQL server instances. Remember, Azure is creating and starting new virtual machines for you under the hood, so it is really doing a lot of work to accommodate your request.

When completed, your account will have one **Mobile Service** and one **SQL database** in addition to the **Default Directory** that is included in all accounts, as shown in the following screenshot:

If you look at the **Scale** tab for your Mobile Service, you'll notice that it is running under the **Free** tier by default. This is a great place for development; at the time of writing this book, it accommodates 500 devices. When deploying your applications into production, you might consider the **Basic** or **Standard** tiers, which also give you the option to add multiple instances.

Creating tables and scripts

The first step to implement a web service in Azure Mobile Services is to create a new table. By default, Azure Mobile Services uses a feature called **dynamic schema** with its SQL database. When you insert a row from the client, new columns are dynamically added to the table. This prevents you from having to create the database schema manually and is a nice code-first approach to developing your backend database. You can always connect to the SQL database manually to fine tune things or make manual changes to the schema.

Return to the management portal, select your mobile services instance, and perform the following steps:

1. Click on the **Data** tab.

2. Click on the **Create** button found at the bottom center of the page.

3. Enter User as the table name.

4. Leave everything else to its default value and click on the **Save** button.

5. Repeat this process to create three more tables named Friend, Message, and Conversation.

Now that we have our four tables, we need to create a script to facilitate the login process for the users in our app. Azure Mobile Services allow you to add custom logic to your tables by creating JavaScript scripts that run in Node.js. You can override what happens to each table during the insert, read, update, or delete operations. In addition, you can also create scripts that are completely freeform if you need other custom logic.

Click on the User table and then click on the **Script** tab. Make sure you are viewing the insert operation. By default, your script will be very simple as seen in the following snippet:

```
function insert(item, user, request) {

    request.execute();

}
```

Scripts in Azure Mobile Services have three parameters, which are stated as follows:

- The item parameter: This is the object that the client sends to the service. In our case, it will be the User object we created in the previous chapters.

- The user parameter: This includes information about the authenticated user. We won't be using this in our examples.

- The request parameter: This is an object used to run the table operation and send a response back to the client. Calling execute will complete the operation and return a successful response to the client.

We need to modify the preceding script to only insert a new user when that user does not already exist. If the user does exist, we need to make sure the password matches the username. Let's make a few changes to the script as shown in the following lines of code:

```
function insert(item, user, request) {
  var users = tables.getTable('user');
  users.where({ username : item.Username }).read({
    success: function(results) {
      if (results.length === 0) {
        //This is a new user
        request.execute();
      }
      else {
        var user = results[0];
        if (item.Password == user.Password) {
          request.respond(statusCodes.OK, user);
        }
        else {
        request.respond(statusCodes.UNAUTHORIZED,
          "Incorrect username or password");
        }
      }
    }
  });
}
```

Let's summarize what we did in the preceding JavaScript:

1. First we grabbed the `user` table. Note that you can reference the name of the table using lower or upper case.

2. Next, we ran a query to pull out any existing users with the `where` function. We used `item.Username`, since this matches our `User` object in C#. Notice how this method is similar to `Linq` in C#.

3. If there are no results, we let the request execute normally.

4. Otherwise, we compare the passwords and return `statusCodes.OK` if they match.

5. If the passwords do not match, we return `statusCodes.UNAUTHORIZED`. This will cause the client to receive an error.

For a complete list of available functions and methods, make sure you check out the server script reference on MSDN at `http://tinyurl.com/AzureMobileServices`.

From here, just make sure you click on the **Save** button to apply your changes. Azure Mobile Services also has the option of providing source control for your scripts via **Git**. Feel free to take advantage of this feature if you want to make changes to the script in your favorite editor locally instead of the website editor.

After this, we need to create one more script. The way XamChat was built earlier in the book, users can add friends by entering their friends' usernames. So in order to insert into the `Friend` table, we will need to modify the `insert` script to look up users by their usernames.

Let's modify the `insert` script for the `Friends` table as follows:

```
function insert(item, user, request) {
  var users = tables.getTable('user');
  users.where({ username : item.Username }).read({
    success: function(results) {
      if (results.length === 0) {
        //Could not find the user
        request.respond(statusCodes.NOT_FOUND,
          "User not found");
      }
      else {
        var existingUser = results[0];
        item.UserId = existingUser.id;
        request.execute();
      }
    }
  });
}
```

This is pretty similar to what we did before; we ran a simple query to load the `user` table based on the `Username` value. We merely have to set the `UserId` value on the new `friend` object prior to the execution of the request.

Adding a backend to XamChat

With our server-side changes complete, the next step is to implement our new service in our XamChat iOS and Android applications. Luckily, as we used an interface named `IWebService`, all we need to do is implement that interface to get it working in our application.

Updating the data types for Azure Mobile Services

Before we begin, it is necessary to go through our existing code and change the data type on the IDs of all our classes from `int` to `string`. This is because the latest version of Azure Mobile Services uses a **GUID (Globally Unique Identifier)**to identify all the objects in its tables. A GUID is a 128-bit unique identifier that can't be expressed as an integer.

Now we can start setting up our service in our iOS application by performing the following steps:

1. Open the `XamChat.iOS` project that we created earlier in the book.
2. Create an `Azure` folder within the `Core` folder.
3. Create a new class named `AzureWebService.cs`.
4. Make the class `public` and implement `IWebService`.
5. Right-click on `IWebService` in your code and select **Refactor | Implement Interface**.
6. A line will appear; press *Enter* to insert the method stubs.

When this setup is complete, your class will look something like the following:

```
public class AzureWebService : IWebService
{
  #region IWebService implementation

  public Task<User> Login(string username, string password)
  {
    throw new NotImplementedException();
  }

  // -- More methods here --

  #endregion
}
```

Adding the Xamarin component

Next, we need to add a reference to the Azure Mobile Services client's .NET library. To do this, we will use the Xamarin Component Store and perform the following:

1. Right-click on the **Components** folder in your iOS project.

2. Click on **Get More Components**.

3. Search for `Azure Mobile Services`, or select it if it is in the featured section.

4. Click on **Add to App**.

> For more information on the Xamarin Component Store, check out *Chapter 9, Third-party Libraries*.

This will download the library and open the following **Getting Started** tab, complete with documentation and samples, in Xamarin Studio:

Close this tab and modify our `AzureWebService.cs` file. Add `using Microsoft.WindowsAzure.MobileServices` to the top of the file, and then make the following changes:

```
public class AzureWebService : IWebService
{
  MobileServiceClient client = new MobileServiceClient(
    "https://your-service-name.azure-mobile.net/",
    "your-application-key");

  public AzureWebService()
  {
    CurrentPlatform.Init();
  }

  // -- Existing code here --
}
```

Make sure you fill in your mobile service name and application key. You can find your key on the **Dashboard** tab of the Azure Management Portal under the **Manage Keys** section. Notice the use of `CurrentPlatform.Init();` calling `MobileServiceClient` will not work properly without calling this first. Our service's constructor is a good location to place this.

Now let's implement our first method, `Login`, in the following manner:

```
public async Task<User> Login(
  string username, string password)
{
  var user = new User
  {
    Username = username,
    Password = password
  };
  await client.GetTable<User>().InsertAsync(user);
  return user;
}
```

This is fairly straightforward, because of how nice this library is to use. The `GetTable<T>` method knows to use a table named `User`, based on the C# class name. Upon the first call, the dynamic schema feature will create two new columns named `Username` and `Password` based on the C# properties of our class. Note that the `InsertAsync` method will also fill in the user's `Id` property for later use in our application.

Next, open the `AppDelegate.cs` file to set up our new service and perform the following:

```
//Replace this line
ServiceContainer.Register<IWebService>(
    () => new FakeWebService());

//With this line
ServiceContainer.Register<IWebService>(
    () => new AzureWebService());
```

Now if you compile and run your application upon log in, your app should successfully call Azure Mobile Services and insert a new user. Navigate to the **Data** tab of your Azure Mobile Service in the Azure Management Portal and select the `User` table. You should see the user you just inserted, as shown in the following screenshot:

user

BROWSE   SCRIPT   COLUMNS   PERMISSIONS

id	Username	Password
0BE66022-52C9-4F67-B17...	jonathanpeppers	password

It is generally a very bad idea to store passwords in plain text in your database. A simple approach to make things a bit more secure would be to store them as a MD5 hash. You should be able to make this change in the custom JavaScript that we are using to insert the password on the User table. A complete guide to securing Windows Azure applications can be found at `http://msdn.microsoft.com/en-us/library/windowsazure/hh696898.aspx`.

Next, let's make a new class named `Friend.cs`. Add it to the `Azure` folder next to the other class specific to Azure as follows:

```
public class Friend
{
    public string Id { get; set; }

    public string MyId { get; set; }

    public string UserId { get; set; }

    public string Username { get; set; }
}
```

We'll use this class to store the friend's information about each user. Note that we also have an `Id` property, and all the classes saved in Azure Mobile Services should have a `string` property named `Id`. This will be the table's primary key in the SQL database.

Next, let's modify the `Message` and `Conversation` classes to prepare for push notifications down the road. Add a new property to the `Message` class as follows:

```
public string ToId { get; set; }
```

Then add the following new property to `Conversation.cs`:

```
public string MyId { get; set; }
```

Here we'll need to insert some test data for our application to function correctly. The easiest way to insert data would be from C#, so let's implement the following simple method on our service to do so:

```
public async Task LoadData()
{
  var users = client.GetTable<User>();
  var friends = client.GetTable<Friend>();

  var me = new User
  {
    Username = "jonathanpeppers",
    Password = "password"
  };
  var friend = new User
  {
    Username = "chucknorris",
    Password = "password"
  };

  await users.InsertAsync(me);
  await users.InsertAsync(friend);

  await friends.InsertAsync(new Friend
    { MyId = me.Id, Username = friend.Username });
  await friends.InsertAsync(new Friend
    { MyId = friend.Id, Username = me.Username });
}
```

Next, let's add the following method to `AppDelegate.cs` and call it from within `FinishedLaunching`:

```
private async void LoadData()
{
  var service = ServiceContainer.Resolve<IWebService>()
    as AzureWebService;

  await service.LoadData();
}
```

If you run your application at this point, it would insert two users and make them friends with each other. Before doing so, let's add some more code to the `LoadData` method to insert conversations and messages as follows:

```
var conversations = client.GetTable<Conversation>();
var messages = client.GetTable<Message>();

var conversation = new Conversation
{
  MyId = me.Id,
  UserId = friend.Id,
  Username = friend.Username,
  LastMessage = "HEY!"
};

await conversations.InsertAsync(conversation);
await messages.InsertAsync(new Message
  { ConversationId = conversation.Id, UserId = friend.Id,
  Username = friend.Username, Text = "What's up?",
  Date = DateTime.Now.AddSeconds(-60),});
await messages.InsertAsync(new Message
  { ConversationId = conversation.Id, UserId = me.Id,
  Username = me.Username, Text = "Not much",
  Date = DateTime.Now.AddSeconds(-30),});
await messages.InsertAsync(new Message
  { ConversationId = conversation.Id, UserId = friend.Id,
  Username = friend.Username, Text = "HEY!",
  Date = DateTime.Now,});
```

Now if you run the application, it will seed the database with some good data to work with. I'd recommend removing the call to `LoadData` once it is successful the first time, and perhaps removing the method entirely when development is complete.

Before going further, let's set up the rest of our `IWebService` interface. It can be implemented as follows:

```
public async Task<User> Register(User user)
{
  await client.GetTable<User>().InsertAsync(user);
  return user;
}

public async Task<User[]> GetFriends(string userId)
{
  var list = await client.GetTable<Friend>()
    .Where(f => f.MyId == userId).ToListAsync();
  return list.Select(f => new User
    { Id = f.UserId, Username = f.Username })
    .ToArray();
}

public async Task<User> AddFriend(
  string userId, string username)
{
  var friend = new Friend
    { MyId = userId, Username = username };
  await client.GetTable<Friend>().InsertAsync(friend);
  return new User { Id = friend.UserId,
    Username = friend.Username };
}
```

Each method here is pretty simple. `Register` is very similar to `Login`, but the main complication for the other methods is the need to convert a `Friend` object to `User`. We used the `ToListAsync` method from the Azure library to get a `List<T>`; however, since our interface uses arrays, we quickly converted the list to an array. We also utilized a couple of basic `Linq` operators such as `Where` and `Select` to accomplish our implementation of `IWebService`.

Now let's complete the methods related to conversations and messages as follows:

```
public async Task<Conversation[]> GetConversations(
  string userId)
{
  var list = await client.GetTable<Conversation>()
    .Where(c => c.MyId == userId).ToListAsync();
  return list.ToArray();
}

public async Task<Message[]> GetMessages(string conversationId)
{
```

```
    var list = await client.GetTable<Message>()
      .Where(m => m.ConversationId == conversationId)
      .ToListAsync();
    return list.ToArray();
  }

  public async Task<Message> SendMessage(Message message)
  {
    await client.GetTable<Message>().InsertAsync(message);
    return message;
  }
}
```

This completes our implementation of `IWebService`. If you run the application at this point, it will function exactly as before with the exception that the app is actually talking to a real web server. New messages will get persisted in the SQL database, and our custom scripts will handle the custom logic that we need. Feel free to play around with our implementation; you might discover some features of Azure Mobile Services that will work great with your own applications.

At this point, another good exercise would be to set up Azure Mobile Services in our Android application. To do so, you will merely need to add the Azure Mobile Services component, a reference to `System.Net.Http.dll`, and link the two new `*.cs` files that we added to the iOS project. After that, you should be able to swap out the `ServiceContainer.Register` call in your `Application` class. Everything will function exactly like on iOS. Isn't cross-platform development great?

Using the Apple Push Notification service

Implementing push notifications with Azure Mobile Services on iOS is very simple to set up from your Azure account's perspective. The most complicated part is working through Apple's process of creating certificates and provisioning profiles in order to configure your iOS application. Before continuing, make sure you have a valid iOS Developer Program account, as you will not be able to send push notifications without it. If you are unfamiliar with the concept of push notifications, take a look at Apple's documentation at `http://tinyurl.com/XamarinAPNS`.

To send push notifications, you need to set up the following:

- An explicit App ID registered with Apple
- A provisioning profile targeting that App ID
- A certificate for your server to trigger the push notification

Apple provides both a development and production certificate, which you can use to send push notifications from your server.

Setting up proper provisioning

Let's begin by navigating to `http://developer.apple.com/account`, and carry out the following steps:

1. Click on the **Identifiers** link.

2. Click on the plus button in the top-right corner of the window.

3. Enter a description, such as `XamChat`, for the bundle ID.

4. Enter your bundle ID under the **Explicit App ID** section. This should match the bundle ID you set up in your `Info.plist` file, for example, `com.yourcompanyname.xamchat`.

5. Under **App Services**, be sure to check **Push Notifications**.

6. Now, click on **Continue**.

7. Review your final settings and hit **Submit**.

This will create an explicit app ID similar to what we can see in the following screenshot, which we can use for sending push notifications:

XamChat		com.jonathanpeppers.xamchat
ID	Name: XamChat	
	Prefix: JVDF6K5T64	
	ID: com.jonathanpeppers.xamchat	

Application Services:

Service	Development	Distribution
Data Protection	Disabled	Disabled
Game Center	Enabled	Enabled
iCloud	Disabled	Disabled
In-App Purchase	Enabled	Enabled
Inter-App Audio	Disabled	Disabled
Passbook	Disabled	Disabled
Push Notifications	Configurable	Configurable

Setting up your provisioning profile

For push notifications, we have to use a profile with an explicit App ID that is not a development certificate. Now let's set up a provisioning profile:

1. Click on the **Development** link under **Provisioning Profiles** in the right-hand side navigation.

2. Click on the plus button in the top-right corner.

3. Check **iOS App Development** and click on **Continue**.

4. Select the App ID we just created and click on **Continue**.

5. Select the developer and click on **Continue**.

6. Select the devices you will be using and click on **Continue**.

7. Enter a name for the profile and click on **Generate**.

8. Download the profile and install it, or open **Xcode** and use the sync button in **Preferences | Accounts**.

When finished successfully, you should arrive at a web page that looks like the following:

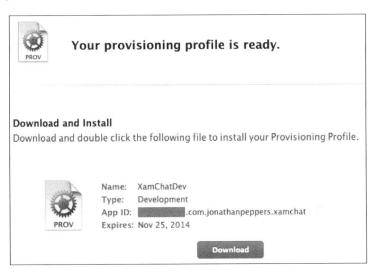

Setting up a certificate signing request

Next, we perform the following steps to set up the certificate our server needs:

1. Click on the **Development** link under **Certificates** in the right-hand side navigation.

2. Click on the plus button in the top-right corner.

3. Enable **Apple Push Notifications service SSL (Sandbox)** and click on **Continue**.

4. Select your App ID as before and click on **Continue**.

5. Create a new certificate signing request as per Apple's instructions. You may also refer to *Chapter 7, Deploying and Testing on Devices*, or locate the `*.certSigningRequest` file created in this chapter.

6. Next, click on **Continue**.

7. Upload the signing request file and click on **Generate**.

8. Next, click on **Download**.

9. Open the file to import the certificate into **Keychain**.

10. Locate the certificate in **Keychain**. It will be titled **Apple Development iOS Push Services** and will contain your bundle ID.

11. Right-click on the certificate and export it somewhere on your filesystem. Enter a password that you would remember.

This will create the certificate we need to send push notifications to our users from Azure Mobile Services. All that remains is to return to the Azure Management Portal and upload the certificate from the **Push** tab under **Apple Push Notification Settings**, as seen in the following screenshot:

This final step concludes the configuration we need from Apple's side.

Making client-side changes for push notifications

Next, let's return to our `XamChat.iOS` project in Xamarin Studio to make the necessary changes on the client side for push notifications. We will need to add a few new classes to our shared code to start with.

Open `IWebService.cs` and add the following new method:

```
Task RegisterPush(string userId, string deviceToken);
```

Next, let's implement this method in `FakeWebService.cs` (just so it compiles) as follows:

```
public async Task RegisterPush( string userId,
  string deviceToken)
{
  await Sleep();
}
```

Now, let's add a new class named `Device.cs` in the `Core/Azure` folder:

```
public class Device
{
  public string Id { get; set;}

  public string UserId { get; set; }

  public string DeviceToken { get; set; }
}
```

Finally, we can implement the real method in `AzureWebService.cs` as follows:

```
public async Task RegisterPush(
  string userId, string deviceToken)
{
  await client.GetTable<Device>()
    .InsertAsync(new Device
    {
      UserId = userId,
      DeviceToken = deviceToken
    });
}
```

As for changes in our ViewModels, we need to add one more new method to `LoginViewModel.cs`:

```
public async Task RegisterPush(string deviceToken)
{
  if (settings.User == null)
```

```
        throw new Exception("User is null");

    await service.RegisterPush(settings.User.Id, deviceToken);
}
```

And then we need to add a small modification to `MessageViewModel.cs`. Add the following line when creating a new `Message` object in the `SendMessage` method:

```
ToId = Conversation.UserId,
```

This modification concludes what we need to add to our shared code. We will reuse this new functionality when we add push notifications to Android, so go ahead and take the time to link in the new `Device.cs` file in your `XamChat.Droid` project to enable you to build your entire solution.

Now, let's add the iOS platform-specific code we need. Add the following methods to your `AppDelegate.cs` file:

```
public async override void RegisteredForRemoteNotifications(
  UIApplication application, NSData deviceToken)
{
  var loginViewModel = ServiceContainer
    .Resolve<LoginViewModel>();
  try
  {
    string token = deviceToken.Description;
    token = token.Substring(1, token.Length - 2);
    await loginViewModel.RegisterPush(token);
  }
  catch (Exception exc)
  {
    Console.WriteLine("Error registering push: " + exc);
  }
}

public override void FailedToRegisterForRemoteNotifications(
  UIApplication application, NSError error)
{
  Console.WriteLine("Error registering push: " +
    error.LocalizedDescription);
}
```

We implemented a couple of important methods in the preceding code snippet. `RegisteredForRemoteNotifications` will occur when Apple successfully returns a device token from its servers. It is returned within angle brackets, so we do a little work to trim those off and pass the device token through the `LoginViewModel` to Azure Mobile Services. We also implemented `FailedToRegisterForRemoteNotifications` just to report any errors that might occur throughout the process.

One last thing to do is to actually make a call to register for remote notifications. Open `LoginController.cs` and add the following line of code directly after the successful call to login:

```
UIApplication.SharedApplication
  .RegisterForRemoteNotificationTypes(
    UIRemoteNotificationType.Alert |
    UIRemoteNotificationType.Badge |
    UIRemoteNotificationType.Sound);
```

You could also call the method on start up; however, in our situation we need a valid user ID to store in the `Device` table in Azure.

Now let's switch to the Azure Management Portal and make the remaining changes on the server side. Under the **Data** tab, create a new table named `Device` with the default settings.

Next, we need to modify the `insert` script so that duplicate device tokens are not inserted:

```
function insert(item, user, request)
{
  var devicesTable = tables.getTable('device');
  devicesTable.where({ userId: item.UserId,
    deviceToken: item.DeviceToken })
    .read({ success: function (devices)
    {
      if (devices.length > 0)
      {
        request.respond(statusCodes.OK, devices[0]);
      }
      else
      {
        request.execute();
      }
    }
  });
}
```

Last but not least, we need to modify the `insert` script for the `Message` table to send push notifications to the user the message was sent to, as follows:

```
function insert(item, user, request) {

    request.execute();

    var devicesTable = tables.getTable('device');
    devicesTable.where({ userId : item.ToId }).read({
      success: function(devices) {
        devices.forEach(function(device) {
          var text = item.Username + ": " + item.Text;
          push.apns.send(device.DeviceToken, {
            alert: text,
            badge: 1,
            payload: {
              message: text
            }
          });
        });
      }
    });
}
```

After executing the request, we retrieve a list of devices from the database and send out a push notification for each one. To test push notifications, deploy the application and log in with the secondary user (if using our examples: `chucknorris`). After logging in, you can just background the app with the home button. Next, log in with the primary user on your iOS simulator and send a message. You should receive a push notification as shown in the following screenshot:

Implementing Google Cloud Messaging

Since we have already set up everything we need in the shared code and on Azure, setting up push notifications for Android will be a lot less work at this time. To continue, you will need a Google account with a verified e-mail address; however, I would recommend using an account registered with **Google Play**, if you have one. You can refer to the full documentation on **Google Cloud Messaging (GCM)** at `http://developer.android.com/google/gcm`.

 Note that Google Cloud Messaging requires that Google Play be installed on the Android device and that the Android OS be at least Version 2.2.

Begin by navigating to `http://cloud.google.com/console` and perform the following steps:

1. Click on the **Create Project** button.
2. Enter an appropriate project name such as `XamChat`.
3. Enter a project ID; you can use the generated one. I prefer to use my application's bundle ID and replace the periods with hyphens.
4. Agree to the **Terms of Service**.
5. Click on the **Create** button.
6. When creating your first project, you may have to verify the mobile number associated with your account.
7. Note the **Project Number** field on the **Overview** page. We will need this number later.

The following screenshot shows the **Overview** tab:

Google Developers Console

‹ XamChat   Project ID: **com-jonathanpeppers-xamchat**   Project Number: 370328391848

Overview

APIs & auth

Permissions

Settings

Support

Welcome. Not sure what to do next?

Now we can continue with our set up as follows:

1. Click on **APIs & auth** in the left-hand side navigation.
2. Scroll down and click on **Google Cloud Messaging for Android**.
3. Click on the **OFF** button at the top to enable the service. You may have to accept another agreement.
4. Click on **Registered Apps** in the left-hand side navigation.
5. Click on the **Register App** button at the top.
6. Enter `XamChat` in the **App Name** field and click on **Register**. You can leave the **Platform** selection on **Web Application** to its default value.
7. Expand the **Server Key** section and copy the **API Key** value to your clipboard.
8. Switch to the Azure Management Portal and navigate to the **Push** tab in your Azure Mobile Service instance.
9. Paste the API key in the **Google Cloud Messaging Settings** section and click on **Save**.

Next, let's modify our `insert` script for the `Message` table to support Android as follows:

```
function insert(item, user, request) {
  request.execute();

  var devicesTable = tables.getTable('device');
  devicesTable.where({ userId : item.ToId }).read({
    success: function(devices) {
      devices.forEach(function(device) {
        if (device.DeviceToken.length > 72) {
          push.gcm.send(device.DeviceToken, {
            title: item.Username,
            message: item.Text,
          });
        }
        else {
          var text = item.Username + ": " + item.Text;
          push.apns.send(device.DeviceToken, {
            alert: text,
            badge: 1,
            payload: {
              message: text
            }
          });
```

```
            }
        });
      }
    });
}
```

Basically, we send any deviceToken values that are longer than 72 characters to GCM. This is one simple way to do it, but you could also add a value to the Device table that indicates if the device is Android or iOS. GCM also supports sending custom values to be displayed in the notification area, so we send an actual title along with the message.

This completes our set up on Azure's side. Setting up the next part in our Android application can be a bit difficult, so we will use a library called **PushSharp** to simplify our implementation.

First, navigate to http://github.com/Redth/PushSharp and perform the following steps:

1. Download the project and place it in the same folder as your XamChat solution.

2. Add the PushSharp.Client.MonoForAndroid.Gcm project to your solution. You can locate the project in the PushSharp.Client subdirectory.

3. Reference the new project from your XamChat.Droid project.

4. If it's not already installed, you will need the **Android SDK Platform** installed for Android 2.2 (API 8). You can install this from the Android SDK manager, launched from the **Tools** menu in Xamarin Studio.

Next, create a new class called PushConstants.cs as follows:

```
public static class PushConstants
{
    public const string BundleId = "your-bundle-id";
    public const string ProjectNumber =
        "your-project-number";
}
```

Fill out the BundleId value with your application's bundle ID and the ProjectNumber value with the project number found on the **Overview** page of your Google Cloud Console.

Next, we need to set up some permissions to support push notifications in our application. Above the namespace declaration in this file, add the following:

```
[assembly: Permission(
  Name = XamChat.Droid.PushConstants.BundleId +
  ".permission.C2D_MESSAGE")]
[assembly: UsesPermission(
  Name = XamChat.Droid.PushConstants.BundleId +
  ".permission.C2D_MESSAGE")]
[assembly: UsesPermission(
  Name = "com.google.android.c2dm.permission.RECEIVE")]
[assembly: UsesPermission(
  Name = "android.permission.GET_ACCOUNTS")]
[assembly: UsesPermission(
  Name = "android.permission.INTERNET")]
[assembly: UsesPermission(
  Name = "android.permission.WAKE_LOCK")]
```

You could also make these changes in our `AndroidManifest.xml` file; however, using C# attributes can be easier since it gives us the ability to use code completion.

Next, create another new class named `PushReceiver.cs` as follows:

```
[BroadcastReceiver(
  Permission = GCMConstants.PERMISSION_GCM_INTENTS)]
[IntentFilter(
  new string[] { GCMConstants.INTENT_FROM_GCM_MESSAGE },
  Categories = new string[] { PushConstants.BundleId })]
[IntentFilter(
  new string[] {
  GCMConstants.INTENT_FROM_GCM_REGISTRATION_CALLBACK },
  Categories = new string[] { PushConstants.BundleId })]
[IntentFilter(
  new string[] {
  GCMConstants.INTENT_FROM_GCM_LIBRARY_RETRY },
  Categories = new string[] { PushConstants.BundleId })]
public class PushReceiver :
  PushHandlerBroadcastReceiverBase<PushHandlerService>
{ }
```

The `PushReceiver.cs` class sets up `BroadcastReceiver`, which is Android's native way for different applications to talk with one another. For more information on the topic, checkout the Android documentation on the subject at `http://developer.android.com/reference/android/content/BroadcastReceiver.html`.

Next, create one last class named `PushService.cs` as follows:

```
[Service]
public class PushHandlerService : PushHandlerServiceBase
{
  public PushHandlerService() :
    base (PushConstants.ProjectNumber)
  {}
}
```

Now, right-click on `PushHandlerServiceBase` and choose **Refactor | Implement abstract members**. Next, let's implement each member one by one:

```
protected async override void OnRegistered (
  Context context, string registrationId)
{
  Console.WriteLine("Push successfully registered!");

  var loginViewModel =
    ServiceContainer.Resolve<LoginViewModel>();
  try
  {
    await loginViewModel.RegisterPush(registrationId);
  }
  catch (Exception exc)
  {
    Console.WriteLine("Error registering push: " + exc);
  }
}
```

This preceding code is very similar to what we did on iOS. We merely have to send the `registrationId` value to `loginViewModel`.

Next, we have to write the following code when the message is received:

```
protected override void OnMessage (
  Context context, Intent intent)
{
  //Pull out the notification details
  string title = intent.Extras.GetString("title");
  string message = intent.Extras.GetString("message");

  //Create a new intent
  intent = new Intent(this, typeof(ConversationsActivity));
```

```
//Create the notification
var notification = new Notification(
  Android.Resource.Drawable.SymActionEmail, title);
notification.Flags = NotificationFlags.AutoCancel;
notification.SetLatestEventInfo(this, title, message,
  PendingIntent.GetActivity(this, 0, intent, 0));

//Send the notification through the NotificationManager
var notificationManager = GetSystemService(
  Context.NotificationService) as NotificationManager;
notificationManager.Notify(1, notification);
}
```

This code will actually pull out the values from the notification and display it in the notification center of the Android device. We used the built-in resource for `SymActionEmail` to display an e-mail icon in the notification.

Next, we just need to implement two more abstract methods. For now, let's just use `Console.WriteLine` to report these events as follows:

```
protected override void OnUnRegistered(
  Context context, string registrationId)
{
  Console.WriteLine("Push unregistered!");
}

protected override void OnError (
  Context context, string errorId)
{
  Console.WriteLine("Push error: " + errorId);
}
```

Down the road, you should consider removing registrations from the `Device` table in Azure when `OnUnRegistered` is called. Occasionally, a user's `registrationId` will change, so this is the place in which your application is notified of this.

Next, open `Application.cs` and add the following lines to the end of `OnCreate`:

```
PushClient.CheckDevice(this);
PushClient.CheckManifest(this);
```

Next, open `LoginActivity.cs` and add the following line after a successful login:

```
PushClient.Register(this, PushConstants.ProjectNumber);
```

Now if you repeat the steps for testing push notifications on iOS, you should be able to send a push notification to our Android app. Even better, you should be able to send push notifications across platforms, since an iOS user could send a message to an Android user.

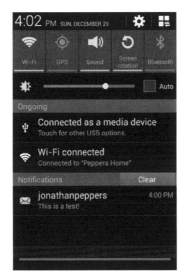

Summary

In this chapter, we went over what Windows Azure provides: Infrastructure as a Service and Platform as a Service. We set up a free Windows Azure account and set up an Azure Mobile Services instance. Next, we created all the tables we needed to store our data and wrote a few scripts to add business logic to the web service. We implemented the client-side code in order to make requests against Azure Mobile Services. Lastly, we implemented push notifications for iOS using the Apple Push Notification service and for Android using Google Cloud Messaging.

Using Azure Mobile Services, we were able to get by without writing much of the server-side code—mainly a few simple scripts. In the next chapter, we'll explore how to use third-party libraries with Xamarin. This includes everything from the Xamarin Component Store to using native Objective-C or Java libraries.

9
Third-party Libraries

Xamarin supports a subset of the .NET framework, but for the most part includes all the standard APIs you would expect in the .NET base class libraries. Because of this, a large portion of C# open source libraries can be used directly in Xamarin projects. Additionally, if an open source project doesn't have a Xamarin or portable class library version, many times porting the code yourself can be very straightforward. Xamarin also supports calling native Objective-C and Java libraries, so we will explore these as additional means of reusing existing code.

In this chapter, we will cover the following:

- The Xamarin Component Store
- Porting existing C# libraries
- Objective-C bindings
- Java bindings

The Xamarin Component Store

The primary and obvious way to add third-party components to your project is via the Xamarin Component Store. The Component Store is fairly similar to **NuGet** on Windows, except that the Component Store also contains premium components that are not free. All Xamarin components are also required to include full sample projects and a getting started guide, while NuGet does not inherently provide documentation in its packages.

All `Xamarin.iOS` and `Xamarin.Android` projects come with a `Components` folder. To get started, simply right-click on the folder and select **Get More Components** to launch the store dialog, as shown in the following screenshot:

At the time of writing this book, there are well over 100 components available to enhance your iOS and Android applications. This is a great place to find the most common components to use within your Xamarin applications. Each component is complete with artwork, possibly a demonstration video, reviews, and other information you would need before purchasing a premium component.

The most well-known and useful components are as follows:

- **Json.NET**: This is the de facto standard for parsing and serializing JSON with C#
- **RestSharp**: This is a commonly used simple REST client for .NET
- **SQLite.NET**: This is a simple **Object Relational Mapper (ORM)** for working with local SQLite databases in your mobile applications
- **Facebook SDK**: This is the standard SDK provided by Facebook for integrating its services into your apps
- **Xamarin.Mobile**: This is a cross-platform library for accessing your device's contacts, GPS, photo library, and camera with a common API
- **ActionBarSherlock**: This is a powerful `ActionBar` replacement for Android

Notice that some of these libraries are native Java or Objective-C libraries, while some are plain C#. Xamarin is built from the ground up to support calling native libraries, so the Component Store offers many of the common libraries that Objective-C or Java developers would leverage when developing mobile applications.

You can also submit your own components to the Component Store. If you have a useful open source project or just want to earn a little extra cash, creating a component is simple. We won't be covering it in this book, but navigate to `http://components.xamarin.com/submit` for full documentation on the subject, as shown in the following screenshot:

Porting existing C# libraries

Even though Xamarin is becoming a popular platform, many open source .NET libraries are simply not up to speed with supporting `Xamarin.iOS` and `Xamarin.Android`. But in these cases, you are definitely not out of luck. Many times, if there is a Silverlight or Windows Phone version of the library, you can simply create an iOS or Android class library and add the files with no code changes.

To help with this process, Xamarin has created an online service tool for scanning your existing code and determining how far off a library is from being portable. Navigate to `http://scan.xamarin.com` and upload any `*.exe` or `*.dll` file to have its methods analyzed for cross-platform development. After the scanning process, you'll get a report of the percentage of how much your component or application is portable to all platforms (Android, iOS, Windows Phone, and Windows Store).

The following screenshot is a sample report of the **SignalR** .NET Client library:

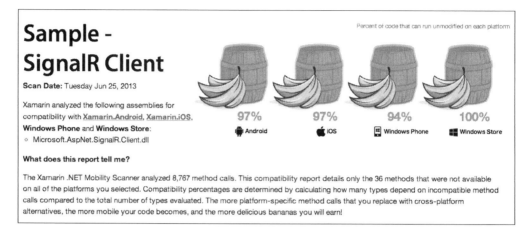

If the library is running a high percentage on portability, you should have a relatively easy time porting it to Android or iOS. In most cases, it can even be easier to port the library to Xamarin than Windows Phone or WinRT.

To illustrate this process, let's port an open source project that doesn't have Xamarin or portable class library support. I have selected a dependency injection library called **Ninject**, due to its usefulness and relationship to ninjas. Find out more about the library at `http://www.ninject.org`.

Let's begin setting up the library to work with Xamarin projects as follows:

1. First, download the source code for Ninject from `https://github.com/ninject/ninject`.

2. Open `Ninject.sln` in Xamarin Studio.

3. Note that the solution does not compile under Mono in Xamarin Studio. That is okay, since we can get it to work for iOS and Android. Ninject has primarily been developed for .NET on Windows and doesn't target Mono on the Mac.

4. Add a new **iOS Library Project** named `Ninject.iOS`.

5. Link in all the files from the `Ninject` main project. Make sure you use the **Add Existing Folder** dialog to speed up this process.

> If you aren't familiar with GitHub, I recommend downloading the desktop client for Mac found at `http://mac.github.com`.

Now try to build the `Ninject.iOS` project; you will get several compiler errors in a file named `DynamicMethodFactory.cs`, as shown in the following screenshot:

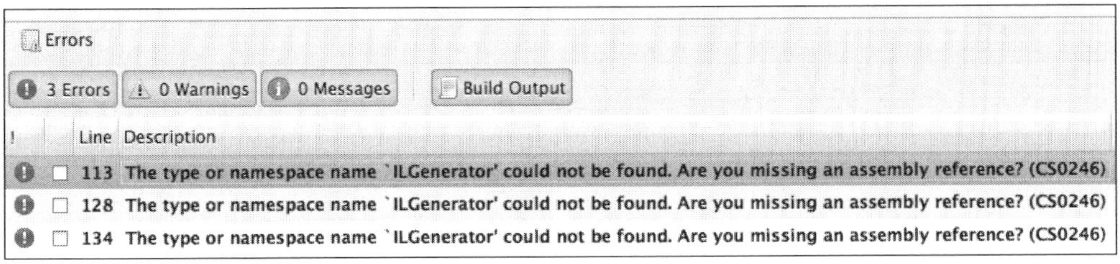

Open `DynamicMethodFactory.cs` and notice the following code at the top of the file:

```
#if !NO_LCG
#region Using Directives
   using System;
   using System.Reflection;
   using System.Reflection.Emit;
   using Ninject.Components;
#endregion

/// *** File contents here ***

#endif
```

It is not possible to use `System.Reflection.Emit` on iOS due to Apple's platform restrictions. Luckily, the library writers have created a preprocessor directive called `NO_LCG` (stands for **Lightweight Code Generation**), to allow the library to run on platforms that do not support `System.Reflection.Emit`.

To fix our iOS project, open the project options and navigate to the **Build | Compiler** section. Add NO_LCG to the **Define Symbols** field for both **Debug** and **Release** in the **Configuration** drop down. Click on **OK** to save your changes. Notice how the entire file is now highlighted with a light gray color in Xamarin Studio as shown in the following screenshot; this means the code will be omitted from being compiled:

```
 1 #region License
 2 //
 3 // Author: Nate Kohari <nate@enkari.com>
 4 // Copyright (c) 2007-2010, Enkari, Ltd.
 5 //
 6 // Dual-licensed under the Apache License, Version 2.0, and the Microsoft Public License (Ms-PL).
 7 // See the file LICENSE.txt for details.
 8 //
 9 #endregion
10 #if !NO_LCG
11 #region Using Directives
12 using System;
13 using System.Reflection;
14 using System.Reflection.Emit;
15 using Ninject.Components;
16 #endregion
17
18 namespace Ninject.Injection
19 {
20     /// <summary>
21     /// Creates injectors for members via <see cref="DynamicMethod"/>s.
22     /// </summary>
23     public class DynamicMethodInjectorFactory : NinjectComponent, IInjectorFactory
24     {
25         /// <summary>
26         /// Gets or creates an injector for the specified constructor.
27         /// </summary>
28         /// <param name="constructor">The constructor.</param>
29         /// <returns>The created injector.</returns>
30         public ConstructorInjector Create(ConstructorInfo constructor)
31         {
32             #if SILVERLIGHT
33             var dynamicMethod = new DynamicMethod(GetAnonymousMethodName(), typeof(object), new[]
34             #else
35             var dynamicMethod = new DynamicMethod(GetAnonymousMethodName(), typeof(object), new[]
36             #endif
37
38             ILGenerator il = dynamicMethod.GetILGenerator();
39
40             EmitLoadMethodArguments(il, constructor);
41             il.Emit(OpCodes.Newobj, constructor);
42
```

If you compile the project now, it will be completed successfully and a Ninject.iOS. dll file will be created, which you can reference from any Xamarin.iOS project. You can also reference the Ninject.iOS project directly instead of using the *.dll file.

At this point, you may wish to repeat the process to create a Xamarin.Android class library project. Luckily, Xamarin.Android supports System.Reflection.Emit, so you can skip adding the additional preprocessor directive if you wish.

Objective-C bindings

Xamarin has developed a sophisticated system for calling native Objective-C libraries from C# in iOS projects. The core of `Xamarin.iOS` uses this same technology to call native Apple APIs in **UIKit**, **CoreGraphics**, and other iOS frameworks. Developers can create iOS binding projects to expose Objective-C classes and methods to C# using simple interfaces and attributes.

To aid in creating Objective-C bindings, Xamarin has created a small tool named **Objective Sharpie** that can process Objective-C header files for you and export the valid C# definitions to add to a binding project. This tool is a great starting point for most bindings that will get your binding three-fourths of the way complete. You will also want to hand edit and fine tune things to be more C# friendly in a lot of cases.

As an example, we will write a binding for the Google Analytics library for iOS. It is a simple and useful library that can track the user activity in your iOS or Android applications. At the time of writing, the version of the Google Analytics SDK was 3.02, so some of these instructions may change as new versions are released.

First download and install Objective Sharpie from `http://tinyurl.com/ ObjectiveSharpie` and perform the following steps:

1. Download the latest Google Analytics SDK for iOS available at `https:// tinyurl.com/GoogleAnalyticsForiOS`.

2. Create a new **iOS Binding Project** named `GoogleAnalytics.iOS`.

3. Run **Objective Sharpie**.

4. Select **iOS 7.0** as the **Target SDK** and click on **Next**.

5. Add all six of the header (`*.h`) files included with the Google Analytics SDK; you can find these in the `Library` folder of the download. Click on **Next**.

6. Pick a suitable namespace such as `GoogleAnalytics` and click on **Generate**.

7. Copy the resulting `ApiDefinition.cs` file that was generated into your iOS binding project.

8. After a few seconds, your C# file will be generated. Click on **Quit**.

When finished, you should have not received any error messages from Objective Sharpie during the process, and your screen should look like the following screenshot:

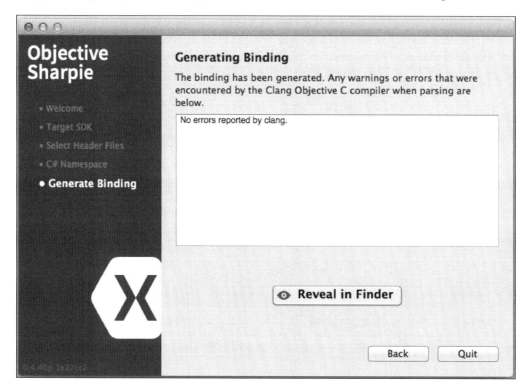

Now if you return to your binding project, you'll notice that Objective Sharpie has generated an interface definition for every class discovered in the header files of the library. It has also generated many enum values that the library uses and changed casing and naming conventions to follow C# more closely where possible.

As you read through the binding, you'll notice several C# attributes that define different aspects about the Objective-C library such as the following:

- BaseType: This declares an interface as an Objective-C class. The base class (also called superclass) is passed in to the attribute. If it has no base class, NSObject should be used.

- Export: This declares a method or property on an Objective-C class. A string that maps the Objective-C name to the C# name is passed in. Objective-C method names are generally in the following form: myMethod:someParam:so meOtherParam.

- Static: This marks a method or property as static in C#.

- `Bind`: This is used on properties to map a getter or setter to a different Objective-C method. Objective-C properties can rename a getter or setter for a property.

- `NullAllowed`: This allows `null` to be passed to a method or property. By default, an exception is thrown if this occurs.

- `Field`: This declares an Objective-C field that is exposed as a public variable in C#.

- `Model`: This identifies a class to `Xamarin.iOS` to have methods that can be optionally overridden. This is generally used on Objective-C delegates.

- `Internal`: This flags the generated member with the C# internal keyword. It can be used to hide certain members that you don't want to expose to the outside world.

- `Abstract`: This identifies an Objective-C method as required, which goes hand in hand with `Model`. In C# it will generate an abstract method.

The only other rule to know is how to define constructors. Xamarin had to invent a convention for this, since C# interfaces do not support constructors.

To define a constructor besides the default one, use the following code:

```
[Export("initWithFrame:")]
IntPtr Constructor(RectangleF frame);
```

This would define a constructor on the class that takes in `RectangleF` as a parameter. The method name, `Constructor`, and the return type, `IntPtr`, signal the Xamarin compiler to generate a constructor.

Now, let's return to our binding project to finish setting up everything. If you compile the project at this point, you'll get a few compiler errors. Let's fix them one by one as follows:

1. Change the default namespace of the project to `GoogleAnalytics`. This setting is found in the project options under **General | Main Settings**.

2. Add `libGoogleAnalyticsServices.a` from the SDK download to the project.

3. Add `using` statements for `MonoTouch.Foundation`, `MonoTouch.UIKit`, and `MonoTouch.ObjCRuntime` at the top of the file.

4. Remove the multiple duplicate declarations of `GAILogLevel`. You may also wish to move any `enumerations` to the `StructsAndEnums.cs` file.

5. Remove the declaration for `GAIErrorCode`.

6. In the `SetAll` method of `GAIDictionaryBuilder`, rename the `params` parameter to `parameters`, as `params` is a reserved word in C#.

7. Remove the duplicate declarations for `GAILogger`, `GAITracker`, and `GAITrackedViewController`.

8. Go through any `Field` declarations and change `[Field("Foobar")]` to `[Field("Foobar", "__Internal")]`. This tells the compiler where the field resides; in this case, it will be included internally in our binding project.

9. Remove all the `Verify` attributes. These are spots where Objective-C Sharpie was unsure of the operation it performed. In our example, all of them are fine; so, it is safe to remove them.

After going through those issues, you should be able to compile the binding and get no errors. You could have read the Objective-C header files and written the definitions yourself by hand; however, using Objective Sharpie generally requires a lot less work.

At this point, if you tried to use the library in an iOS project, you would get an error such as the following:

```
Error MT5210: Native linking failed, undefined symbol:

  _FooBar. Please verify that all the necessary frameworks

  have been referenced and native libraries are properly

  linked in.
```

We need to define the other frameworks and libraries that the Objective-C library uses. This is very similar to how references work in C#. If we review the Google Analytics documentation, it says that you must add `CoreData`, `SystemConfiguration`, and `libz.dylib`. Additionally, you must add a weak reference to `AdSupport`.

Open `libGoogleAnalyticsServices.linkwith.cs` that was created automatically nested underneath the `*.a` file and make the following changes:

```
[assembly: LinkWith ("libGoogleAnalyticsServices.a",
  LinkTarget.ArmV7 | LinkTarget.ArmV7s | LinkTarget.Simulator,
  LinkerFlags = "-lz",
  Frameworks = "CoreData SystemConfiguration",
  WeakFrameworks = "AdSupport",
  ForceLoad = true)]
```

We added references to frameworks in the following ways:

* **Frameworks**: Add them to the `Frameworks` value on the `LinkWith` attribute, delimited by spaces.

- **Weak Frameworks**: Add them to the `WeakFrameworks` property on the `LinkWith` attribute in the same manner. Weak frameworks are libraries that can be ignored if they are not found. In this case, `AdSupport` was added in iOS 6; however, this library will still work on older versions of iOS.

- **Dynamic Libraries**: Libraries such as `libz.dylib`; can be declared in `LinkerFlags`. Generally, you drop the `.dylib` extension and replace `lib` with `-l`.

After these changes are implemented, you will be able to successfully use the library from iOS projects. For complete documentation on Objective-C bindings, visit the Xamarin documentation site at `http://docs.xamarin.com/ios`.

Java bindings

In the same manner as iOS, Xamarin has provided full support for calling into Java libraries from C# with `Xamarin.Android`. The native Android SDKs function in this way and developers can leverage the `Android Java Bindings` project to take advantage of other native Java libraries in C#. The main difference here is that not a lot has to be done by hand in comparison to Objective-C bindings. The Java syntax is very similar to that of C#; so many mappings are exactly one-to-one. In addition, Java has metadata information included with its libraries, which Xamarin uses to automatically generate the C# code required for calling into Java.

As an example, let's make a binding for the Android version of the Google Analytics SDK. Before we begin, download the SDK at `http://tinyurl.com/GoogleAnalyticsForAndroid`. At the time of writing, the version of the Android SDK was 3.01, so some of these instructions may change over time.

Let's begin creating a Java binding as follows:

1. Start a new `Android Java Bindings Library` project in Xamarin Studio. You may use the same solution as we did for iOS if you wish.

2. Name the project `GoogleAnalytics.Droid`.

3. Add `libGoogleAnalyticsServices.jar` from the Android SDK to the project under the `Jars` folder.

4. Build the project. You will get a few errors, which we'll address in a moment.

Most of the time you spend working on Java bindings will be to fix small issues that prevent the generated C# code from compiling. But don't fret; a lot of libraries will work on the first try without having to make any changes at all. Generally, the larger the Java library is, the more work you have to do to get it working from C#.

The following are the types of issues you may run into:

- **Java obfuscation**: If the library is run through an obfuscation tool such as **ProGuard**, the class and method names may not be valid C# names.

- **Covariant return types**: Java has different rules for return types than C# does. A class can override a method from its subclass and change the return type to a subclass of that type. For this reason, you may need to modify the return type for the generated C# code to compile.

- **Visibility**: The rules that Java has for accessibility are different from those of C#; the visibility of methods in subclasses can be changed. Sometimes you will have to change visibility in C# to get it to compile.

- **Naming collisions**: Sometimes the C# code generator can get things a bit wrong and generate two members or classes with the same name.

- **Java generics**: The use of generic classes in Java can often cause issues in C#.

So before we get started on solving these issues in our Java binding, let's first clean up the namespaces in the project. Java namespaces are of the form `com.mycompany.mylibrary` by default, so let's change the definition to match C# more closely. In the `Transforms` directory of the project, open `Metadata.xml` and add the following XML tag inside the root metadata node:

```
<attr path="/api/package[@name='com.google.analytics.tracking
    .android']" name="managedName">GoogleAnalytics.Tracking</attr>
```

The `attr` node tells the Xamarin compiler what needs to be replaced in the Java definition with another value. In this case, we are replacing `managedName` of the package with `GoogleAnalytics.Tracking` because it will make much more sense in C#. The path value may look a bit strange, which is because it is using an XML matching query language named **XPath**. In general, just think of it as pattern - matching for XML. For full documentation on XPath syntax, check out some of the many resources online such as `http://w3schools.com/xpath`.

You may be asking yourself at this point, what is the XPath expression matching against? Return to Xamarin Studio and right-click on the solution at the top. Click on **Display Options | Show All Files**. Open `api.xml` under the `obj/Debug` folder. This is the Java definition file that describes all types and methods within the Java library. If you notice, the XML here directly correlates to the XPath expressions we'll be writing.

For our next step, let's remove all the packages (or namespaces) we don't plan on using in this library. This is generally a good idea for large libraries, since you don't want to waste time fixing issues with parts of the library you won't even be calling from C#. Note that it doesn't actually remove the Java code; it just prevents the generation of the C# code necessary for calling into the Java library.

Add the following declarations in `Metadata.xml`:

```
<remove-node
  path="/api/package[@name='com.google.analytics
  .containertag.common']" />
<remove-node
  path="/api/package[@name='com.google.analytics
  .containertag.proto']" />
<remove-node
  path="/api/package[@name='com.google.analytics
  .midtier.proto.containertag']" />
<remove-node
  path="/api/package[@name='com.google.android
  .gms.analytics.internal']" />
<remove-node
  path="/api/package[@name='com.google.android
  .gms.common.util']" />
<remove-nodepath="/api/package[@name='com.google.tagmanager']" />
<remove-node
  path="/api/package[@name='com.google.tagmanager.proto']" />
<remove-node
  path="/api/package[@name='com.google.tagmanager.protobuf']" />
```

Now when you build the library, we can start resolving issues. The first error you will receive will be something like the following:

```
GoogleAnalytics.Tracking.GoogleAnalytics.cs(74,74):
    Error CS0234: The type or namespace name `TrackerHandler'
    does not exist in the namespace `GoogleAnalytics.Tracking'.
    Are you missing an assembly reference?
```

If we locate `TrackerHandler` within the `api.xml` file, we'll see the following class declaration:

```
<class
  abstract="true" deprecated="not deprecated"
  extends="java.lang.Object"
  extends-generic-aware="java.lang.Object"
  final="false" name="TrackerHandler"
  static="false" visibility=""/>
```

So, can you spot the problem? We need to fill out the `visibility` XML attribute, which for some reason is blank. Add the following line to `Metadata.xml`:

```
<attr
  path="/api/package[@name='com.google.analytics
  .tracking.android']/class[@name='TrackerHandler']"
  name="visibility">public</attr>
```

This XPath expression will locate the `TrackerHandler` class inside the `com.google.analytics.tracking.android` package and change `visibility` to `public`.

If you build the project now, it will complete successfully with one warning. In Java binding projects, it is a good idea to fix warnings, since they generally indicate that a class or method is being omitted from the binding. Notice the following warning:

```
GoogleAnalytics.Droid: Warning BG8102:
    Class GoogleAnalytics.Tracking.CampaignTrackingService has
    unknown base type android.app.IntentService (BG8102)
    (GoogleAnalytics.Droid)
```

To fix this issue, locate the type definition for `CampaignTrackingService` in `api.xml`, which would be as follows:

```
<class
  abstract="false" deprecated="not deprecated"
  extends="android.app.IntentService"
  extends-generic-aware="android.app.IntentService"
  final="false" name="CampaignTrackingService"
  static="false" visibility="public">
```

The way to fix the issue here is to change the base class to the `Xamarin.Android` definition for `IntentService`. Add the following code to `Metadata.xml`:

```
<attr
  path="/api/package[@name='com.google.analytics
  .tracking.android']/class[@name='CampaignTrackingService']"
  name="extends">mono.android.app.IntentService</attr>
```

This changes the `extends` attribute to use the `IntentService` found in `Mono.Android.dll`. I located the Java name for this class by opening `Mono.Android.dll` in Xamarin Studio's **Assembly Browser** and looking at the `Register` attribute, as shown in the following screenshot:

To inspect the `*.dll` files in Xamarin Studio, you merely have to open them. You can also double-click on any assembly in the `References` folder in your project.

If you build the binding project now, we're left with one last error as follows:

```
GoogleAnalytics.Tracking.CampaignTrackingService.cs(24,24):
    Error CS0507:
    `CampaignTrackingService.OnHandleIntent(Intent)':
    cannot change access modifiers when overriding `protected'
    inherited member
    `IntentService.OnHandleIntent(Android.Content.Intent)'
    (CS0507) (GoogleAnalytics.Droid)
```

If you navigate to the `api.xml` file, you can see the definition for `OnHandleIntent` as follows:

```
<method
    abstract="false" deprecated="not deprecated" final="false"
    name="onHandleIntent" native="false" return="void"
    static="false" synchronized="false" visibility="public">
```

We can see here that the Java method for this class is `public`, but the base class is `protected`. So the best way to fix this is to change the C# version to `protected` as well. Writing an XPath expression to match this is a bit more complicated, but luckily Xamarin has an easy way to retrieve it. If you double-click on the error message in the **Errors** pad of Xamarin Studio, you'll see the following comment in the generated C# code:

```
// Metadata.xml XPath method reference:
    path="/api/package[@name='com.google.analytics
    .tracking.android']/class[@name='CampaignTrackingService']
    /method[@name='onHandleIntent' and count(parameter)=1 and
    parameter[1][@type='android.content.Intent']]"
```

Copy this value for `path`, and add the following to `Metadata.xml`:

```
<attr path="/api/package[@name='com.google.analytics
    .tracking.android']/class[@name='CampaignTrackingService']
    /method[@name='onHandleIntent' and count(parameter)=1 and
    parameter[1][@type='android.content.Intent']]"
    name="visibility">protected</attr>
```

Now, we can build the project and get zero errors and zero warnings. The library is now ready for use within your `Xamarin.Android` projects.

However, if you start working with the library, notice how the parameter names for methods are p0, p1, p2, and so on. Here are a few method definitions of the EasyTracker class:

```
public static EasyTracker GetInstance(Context p0);
public static void SetResourcePackageName(string p0);
public virtual void ActivityStart(Activity p0);
public virtual void ActivityStop(Activity p0);
```

You can imagine how difficult it could be to consume a Java library without knowing the proper parameter names. The reason the parameters are named this way is because the Java metadata for its libraries does not include the information to set the proper name for each parameter. So, Xamarin.Android does the best thing it can and automatically names each parameter sequentially.

To rename the parameters in this class, we can add the following to Metadata.xml:

```
<attr path="/api/package[@name='com.google.analytics
  .tracking.android']/class[@name='EasyTracker']
  /method[@name='getInstance']/parameter[@name='p0']"
  name="name">context</attr>
<attr path="/api/package[@name='com.google.analytics
  .tracking.android']/class[@name='EasyTracker']
  /method[@name='setResourcePackageName']/parameter[@name='p0']"
  name="name">packageName</attr>
<attr path="/api/package[@name='com.google.analytics
  .tracking.android']/class[@name='EasyTracker']
  /method[@name='activityStart']/parameter[@name='p0']"
  name="name">activity</attr>
<attr path="/api/package[@name='com.google.analytics
  .tracking.android']/class[@name='EasyTracker']
  /method[@name='activityStop']/parameter[@name='p0']"
  name="name">activity</attr>
```

Upon rebuilding the binding project, this will effectively rename the parameters for these four methods in the EasyTracker class. At this time, I would recommend going through the classes you plan on using in your application and rename the parameters so that it will make more sense to you. You might need to refer to the Google Analytics documentation to get the naming correct. Luckily, there is a javadocs.zip file included in the SDK that provides HTML reference for the library.

For a full reference on implementing Java bindings, make sure to check out Xamarin's documentation site at http://docs.xamarin.com/android. There are certainly more complicated scenarios than what we ran into for creating a binding for the Google Analytics library.

Summary

In this chapter, we added libraries from the Xamarin Component Store to Xamarin projects and ported an existing C# library, Ninject, to both `Xamarin.iOS` and `Xamarin.Android`. Next, we installed Objective Sharpie and explored its usage for generating Objective-C bindings. Finally, we wrote a functional Objective-C binding for the Google Analytics SDK for iOS and a Java binding for the Google Analytics SDK for Android. We also wrote several XPath expressions to clean up the Java binding.

There are several available options for using existing third-party libraries from your `Xamarin.iOS` and `Xamarin.Android` applications. We looked at everything from using the Xamarin Component Store, porting existing code, and setting up Java and Objective-C libraries to be used from C#. In the next chapter, we will cover the `Xamarin.Mobile` library as a way to access a user's contacts, camera, and GPS location.

10
Contacts, Camera, and Location

Some of the most vital features used by mobile applications today are based on the new types of data that can be collected by our devices. Features such as GPS location and camera are staples in modern applications such as Instagram or Twitter. It's difficult to develop an application and not use some of these functionalities. So, let's explore our options to take advantage of these new types of data with Xamarin.

In this chapter, we will do the following:

- Introduce the Xamarin.Mobile library
- Read the address book on Android and iOS
- Retrieve the GPS location of our device
- Pull photos from the camera and photo library

Introducing Xamarin.Mobile

To simplify the development of these features across multiple platforms, Xamarin has developed a library called **Xamarin.Mobile**. It delivers a single API for accessing the contacts, GPS location, cardinal direction, camera, and photo library for iOS, Android, and even Windows platforms. It also takes advantage of **Task Parallel Libraries (TPL)** to deliver a modern C# API that will make developers more productive than what their native alternatives would. This gives you the ability to write nice, clean, asynchronous code using the `async` and `await` keywords in C#. You can also reuse the same code in iOS and Android, minus a few differences that are required by the Android platform.

To install Xamarin.Mobile, open the **Xamarin Component Store** in **Xamarin Studio** and add the **Xamarin.Mobile** component to a project, as shown in the following screenshot; you're going to be using these features (of the component):

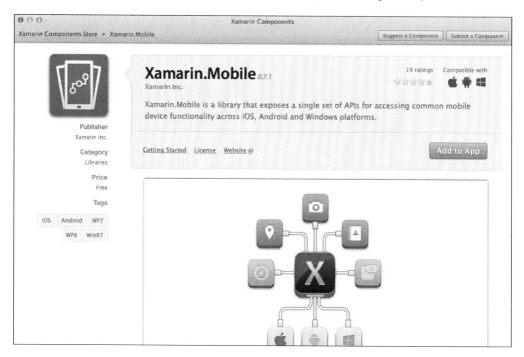

Before we dig further into using Xamarin.Mobile, let's review the namespaces and functionalities available with the library:

- `Xamarin.Contacts`: This contains classes classes that enable you to interact with the full address book. It includes everything from the contact's photo, phone numbers, address, e-mail, website, and so on.

- `Xamarin.Geolocation`: This combined with the accelerometer gives you access to the device's GPS location including the altitude, heading, longitude, latitude, and speed. You can track the device's position explicitly or listen for GPS position changes over time.

- `Xamarin.Media`: This grants access to the device's camera (or cameras if there are more than one) and built-in photo library. This is an easy way to add photo selection capabilities to any application.

For the full documentation of Xamarin.Mobile, visit the API documentation included with the Component Store at `http://componentsapi.xamarin.com`. You can also view it in the native Mono documentation browser by clicking on **Open API Documentation** when viewing the component in Xamarin Studio.

Xamarin.Mobile is also an open source project with the standard Apache 2.0 license. You can contribute to the project or submit issues to the GitHub page at `https://github.com/xamarin/Xamarin.Mobile`. Feel free to use Xamarin.Mobile in your applications, or fork and modify it for your own purposes.

Accessing contacts

To begin our exploration of what Xamarin.Mobile offers, let's access the address book within a Xamarin application. For iOS, the first step is to make a **Single View Application** project by navigating to **iOS | iPhone Storyboard**. Make sure you add Xamarin.Mobile to the project from the Component Store.

Now, let's implement a simple `UITableView` with a list of contacts:

1. Open the `MainStoryboard.storyboard` file. Delete any existing controllers created by the project template.

2. Create `UINavigationController` with `UITableViewController` as its root child controller.

3. Set the class of `UITableViewController` to `ContactsController` found under **Identity Inspector** in Xcode.

4. Save the storyboard file and return to Xamarin Studio.

Open the automatically generated `ContactsController.cs` file and start implementing the table view. Add `using Xamarin.Contact,` to the top of the file, and make the following changes to the controller:

```
public partial class ContactsController :
  UITableViewController, IUITableViewDataSource
{
  public ContactsController (IntPtr handle) : base (handle)
  {
    Title = "Contacts";
  }
}
```

We filled out the title for the navigation bar, `"Contacts,"` and set the class to implement `IUITableViewDataSource`. This is a new type of interface that Xamarin has created to simplify using Objective-C protocols from C#. It is the exact same as creating a class that inherits from `UITableViewSource`, as we did in earlier chapters, but you can do it from your controller as well. Xamarin has done some tricks here. They have created an interface with methods that can be optionally implemented, which isn't something that C# supports. This type of interface can make your code a bit cleaner by reducing the need for a new class, which is great for very simple controllers.

Next, let's add some code to load the contacts:

```
Contact[] contacts;

public async override void ViewDidLoad()
{
  base.ViewDidLoad();
  try
  {
    var book = new AddressBook();
    await book.RequestPermission();
    contacts = book.ToArray();
  }
  catch
  {
    new UIAlertView("Oops!",
      "Something went wrong, try again later.",
      null, "Ok").Show();
  }
}
```

To use Xamarin.Mobile for loading contacts, you must first create an `AddressBook` object. Next, we have to call `RequestPermissions` in order to ask the user for permission to access the address book. This is an important step since it is required by iOS devices before an application can access the user's contacts. This prevents potentially nefarious applications from retrieving contacts without the user's knowledge.

Next, we used the `System.Linq` extension method `ToArray` to enumerate over the address book and store it in member variable named contacts. You can also `foreach` over the `AddressBook` object depending on your needs.

If you were to compile and run the application at this point, you would be greeted by the standard iOS pop up requesting access to contacts, as shown in the following screenshot:

If you accidentally hit **Don't Allow**, you can change this setting by navigating to **Settings | Privacy | Contacts** on the device. In the iOS Simulator, you can also reset all privacy prompts in the simulator by closing the application and going to **Settings | General | Reset | Reset Location & Privacy**.

So for the next step, we'll need to implement the `IUITableViewDataSource` interface so that we can work with the array of contacts and display them on the screen. Add the following methods to the controller just like you would to `UITableViewSource`:

```
public override int RowsInSection(
  UITableView tableview, int section)
{
  return contacts != null ? contacts.Length : 0;
}
public override UITableViewCell GetCell(
  UITableView tableView, NSIndexPath indexPath)
{
  var contact = contacts [indexPath.Row];
  var cell = tableView.DequeueReusableCell(CellName);
  if (cell == null)
    cell = new UITableViewCell(
      UITableViewCellStyle.Default, CellName);
    cell.TextLabel.Text =
      contact.LastName + ", " + contact.FirstName;
    return cell;
}
```

Also, add a `CellName` constant string to the class by selecting a string identifier such as `ContactCell`. Now if you compile and run the program, you'll be able to see the list of contacts on the device. The following screenshot shows the default list of contacts in the iOS 7 Simulator:

Retrieving contacts on Android

In a very similar fashion, we can retrieve a list of contacts in Android with Xamarin. Mobile. All of the APIs in Xamarin.Mobile are identical in Android with the exception of the requirement that Android.Content.Context be passed in a few places. This is because many native Android APIs require a reference to the current activity (or to an other context such as Application) in order to function properly. To begin, create a standard Android Application project by navigating to **Android | Android Application** in Xamarin Studio. Make sure to add Xamarin.Mobile to the project from the Component Store.

In parallel to iOS, let's create ListView to display a list of contacts as follows:

1. Open the Main.axml file from the layout folder under the Resources directory in the Android designer.

2. Remove the default button from the project template and add **ListView** to the layout.

3. Set **Id** to @+id/contacts.

4. Save the file and open MainActivity.cs so we can make some changes to the code.

Begin by removing most of the code; we don't need the code that came from the project template. You will also need to add a using statement for Xamarin. Contacts. Next, let's implement BaseAdapter<Contact> inside the MainActivity class as follows:

```
class ContactsAdapter : BaseAdapter<Contact>
{
  public Contact[] Contacts { get; set; }
  public override long GetItemId(int position)
  {
    return position;
  }
  public override View GetView(
    int position, View convertView, ViewGroup parent)
  {
    var contact = this [position];
    var textView = convertView as TextView;
    if (textView == null)
    {
      textView = new TextView(parent.Context);
    }
    textView.Text = contact.LastName + ", " + contact.FirstName;
    return textView;
```

```
    }
    public override int Count
    {
      get { return Contacts == null ? 0 : Contacts.Length; }
    }
    public override Contact this[int index]
    {
      get { return Contacts [index]; }
    }
  }
```

This will display each contact in `TextView` for each row in the `ListView`. One thing that we've done here in order to simplify things is add a property for the array of contacts. This should be pretty straightforward and similar to what we've done in past chapters.

Now, let's set up the adapter in `OnCreate` as follows:

```
protected async override void OnCreate(Bundle bundle)
{
  base.OnCreate(bundle);
  SetContentView(Resource.Layout.Main);
  var listView = FindViewById<ListView>(Resource.Id.contacts);
  var adapter = new ContactsAdapter();
  listView.Adapter = adapter;
  try
  {
    var book = new AddressBook(this);
    await book.RequestPermission();
    adapter.Contacts = book.ToArray();
    adapter.NotifyDataSetChanged();
  }
  catch
  {
    new AlertDialog.Builder(this).SetTitle("Oops")
      .SetMessage("Something went wrong, try again later.")
      .SetPositiveButton("Ok", delegate { }).Show();
  }
}
```

This code calling Xamarin.Mobile is identical to what we did on the code for iOS except here, `this` had to be passed for the Android `Context` in the constructor for `AddressBook`. Our code changes are complete; however, if you ran the application right now, an exception would be thrown. Android requires permission in the manifest file, which will notify the user of its access to the address book when it is downloaded from Google Play.

We must create an `AndroidManifest.xml` file and declare one permission as follows:

1. Open the project options for the Android project.
2. Select the **Android Application** tab under **Build**.
3. Click on **Add Android manifest**.
4. Under the **Required permissions** section, check **ReadContacts**.
5. Click on **OK** to save your changes.

Now if you run the application, you will get a list of all the contacts on the device, as shown in the following screenshot:

Looking up GPS location

Using Xamarin.Mobile to track a user's GPS location is as simple as accessing their contacts. There is a similar process for setting up access on iOS and Android, but in the case of location, you don't have to request permission using code. iOS will automatically show the standard alert requesting permission, and Android requires a manifest setting.

As an example, let's create an application that displays a list of GPS location updates over time. Let's begin with an iOS example by creating a Single View Application project. This can be done by navigating to **iOS | iPhone Storyboard** and clicking on **Single View Application**, just like in the previous section. Make sure you add Xamarin.Mobile to the project from the Component Store.

Now, let's implement `UITableView` to display a list of GPS updates as follows:

1. Open the `MainStoryboard.storyboard` file. Delete any existing controllers created by the project template.

2. Create `UINavigationController` with `UITableViewController` as its root child controller.

3. Set the class of `UITableViewController` to `LocationController` found under the **Identity Inspector** in Xcode.

4. Save the storyboard file and return to Xamarin Studio.

Open `LocationController.cs` and let's start by setting up our GPS to update a table view over time. Add `using Xamarin.Geolocation;` to the top of the file; we can set up some member variables and create our `Geolocator` object in the controller's constructor as follows:

```
Geolocator locator;
List<string> messages = new List<string>();
public LocationController (IntPtr handle) : base (handle)
{
  Title = "GPS";
  locator = new Geolocator();
  locator.PositionChanged += OnPositionChanged;
  locator.PositionError += OnPositionError;
}
```

Next, we can set up our event handlers as follows:

```
void OnPositionChanged (object sender, PositionEventArgs e)
{
  messages.Add(string.Format("Long: {0:0.##} Lat: {1:0.##}",
    e.Position.Longitude, e.Position.Latitude));
  TableView.ReloadData();
}
void OnPositionError (object sender, PositionErrorEventArgs e)
{
  messages.Add(e.Error.ToString());
  TableView.ReloadData();
}
```

These will add a message to the list when there is an error or a location change. We used `string.Format` to only display the longitude and latitude up to two decimal places.

Next, we have to actually tell `Geolocator` to start listening for GPS updates. We can do this in `ViewDidLoad` as follows:

```
public override void ViewDidLoad()
{
  base.ViewDidLoad();
  locator.StartListening(1000, 50);
}
```

In the preceding code, `1000` is a hint for the minimum time to update the GPS location, and the value `50` is a hint for the number of meters that will trigger a position update.

Last but not least, we need to set up the table view. Set up `LocationController` to implement `IUITableViewDataSource` and add the following methods to the controller:

```
public override int RowsInSection(
  UITableView tableview, int section)
{
  return messages.Count;
}
public override UITableViewCell GetCell(
  UITableView tableView, NSIndexPath indexPath)
{
  var cell = tableView.DequeueReusableCell(CellName);
  if (cell == null)
    cell = new UITableViewCell(
      UITableViewCellStyle.Default, CellName);
  cell.TextLabel.Text = messages [indexPath.Row];
  return cell;
}
```

If you compile and run the application, you should see an iOS permission prompt followed by the longitude and latitude in the table view over time, as shown in the following screenshot:

Implementing GPS location on Android

Just as in the previous section, using Xamarin.Mobile for GPS location is almost identical to the APIs we used in iOS. To begin with our Android example, go to **Android | Android Application** in Xamarin Studio. Make sure you add Xamarin. Mobile to the project from the Component Store.

Let's create `ListView` to display a list of messages of the GPS location updates as follows:

1. Open the `Main.axml` file from the `layout` folder under the `Resources` directory in the Android designer.

2. Remove the default button from the project template and add `ListView` to the layout.

3. Set **Id** to `@+id/messages`.

4. Save the file and open `MainActivity.cs` so that we can make some code changes.

As usual, remove any extra code that was created by the project template. Next, add a `using` statement for `Xamarin.Geolocation`. Then, add a simple `BaseAdapter<string>` inside the `MainActivity` class as follows:

```
class Adapter : BaseAdapter<string>
{
  List<string> messages = new List<string>();
  public void Add(string message)
  {
    messages.Add(message);
    NotifyDataSetChanged();
  }
  public override long GetItemId(int position)
  {
    return position;
  }
  public override View GetView(
    int position, View convertView, ViewGroup parent)
  {
    var textView = convertView as TextView;
    if (textView == null)
      textView = new TextView(parent.Context);
    textView.Text = messages [position];
    return textView;
  }
  public override int Count
```

```
  {
    get { return messages.Count; }
  }
  public override string this[int index]
  {
    get { return messages [index]; }
  }
}
```

This is similar to other Android adapters we have set up in the past. One difference here is that we made a member variable that contains a List<string> of messages and a method to add new messages to the list.

Now, let's add a few methods to the MainActivity class in order to set up the GPS location updates as follows:

```
Geolocator locator;
Adapter adapter;
protected override void OnCreate(Bundle bundle)
{
  base.OnCreate(bundle);
  SetContentView(Resource.Layout.Main);
  var listView = FindViewById<ListView>(Resource.Id.messages);
  listView.Adapter =
    adapter = new Adapter();
  locator = new Geolocator(this);
  locator.PositionChanged += OnPositionChanged;
  locator.PositionError += OnPositionError;
}

protected override void OnResume()
{
  base.OnResume();
  locator.StartListening(1000, 50);
}
protected override void OnPause()
{
  base.OnPause();
  locator.StopListening();
}
void OnPositionChanged (object sender, PositionEventArgs e)
{
  adapter.Add(string.Format("Long: {0:0.##} Lat: {1:0.##}",
    e.Position.Longitude, e.Position.Latitude));
}
```

```
void OnPositionError (object sender, PositionErrorEventArgs e)
{
  adapter.Add(e.Error.ToString());
}
```

Again, this looks identical to the code for iOS except for the constructor for `Geolocator`. If you ran the application at this point, it would start with no errors. However, no events would be fired from the `Geolocator` object. We first need to add permission to access the location from the Android Manifest file. It is also a good idea to start the locator in `OnResume` and stop it in `OnPause`. This will conserve battery by stopping the GPS location when this activity is no longer on the screen.

Let's create an `AndroidManifest.xml` file and declare two permissions as follows:

1. Open the project options for the Android project.
2. Select the **Android Application** tab under **Build**.
3. Click on **Add Android manifest**.
4. Under the **Required permissions** section, check **AccessCoarseLocation** and **AccessFineLocation**.
5. Click on **OK** to save your changes.

Now if you compile and run the application, you will get the GPS location updates over time as shown in the following screenshot:

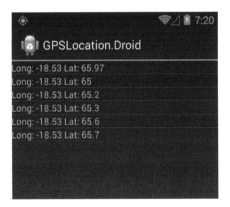

Accessing the photo library and camera

The last major feature of Xamarin.Mobile is the ability to access photos in order to give users the ability to add their own content to your applications. Using a class called `MediaPicker`, you can pull photos from the device's camera or photo library and optionally display your own UI for the operation.

Let's create an application that loads an image from the camera or photo library on the press of a button and displays it on the screen. To begin with, create a Single View Application project by going to **iOS** | **iPhone Storyboard** | **Single View Application** in Xamarin Studio. Make sure you add Xamarin.Mobile to the project from the Component Store.

Now, let's implement a screen with two `UIButtons` and a `UIImageView` as follows:

1. Open the `MainStoryboard.storyboard` file. Delete any existing controllers created by the project template.

2. Create `UIViewController` with one `UIImageView` and two `UIButtons` named `Library` and `Camera`.

3. Set the class of `UITableViewController` to `ContactsController`, found under the **Identity Inspector** in Xcode.

4. Create outlets for each view in the controller named `imageView`, `library`, and `camera` respectively.

5. Save the storyboard file and return to Xamarin Studio.

Now, open `PhotoController.cs` and add the following code in `ViewDidLoad`:

```
MediaPicker picker;
public override void ViewDidLoad()
{
  base.ViewDidLoad();
  picker = new MediaPicker();
  if (!picker.IsCameraAvailable)
    camera.Enabled = false;
  camera.TouchUpInside += OnCamera;
  library.TouchUpInside += OnLibrary;
}
```

Note that we have to check `IsCameraAvailable` and disable the `camera` button. There are iOS devices such as the first generation iPad that could possibly not have a camera. Besides this, we just need to create an instance of `MediaPicker` that can be used when each button is clicked.

Now, let's add a method for each button's `TouchUpInside` event and a couple of other helper methods as follows:

```
async void OnCamera (object sender, EventArgs e)
{
  try
  {
    var file = await picker.TakePhotoAsync(
```

```
      new StoreCameraMediaOptions());
    imageView.Image = ToImage(file);
  }
  catch
  {
    ShowError();
  }
}
async void OnLibrary (object sender, EventArgs e)
{
  try
  {
    var file = await picker.PickPhotoAsync();
    imageView.Image = ToImage(file);
  }
  catch
  {
    ShowError();
  }
}
UIImage ToImage(MediaFile file)
{
  using (var stream = file.GetStream())
  {
    using (var data = NSData.FromStream(stream))
    {
      return UIImage.LoadFromData(data);
    }
  }
}
void ShowError()
{
  new UIAlertView("Oops!",
    "Something went wrong, try again later.", null, "Ok").Show();
}
```

Using `MediaPicker` is pretty straightforward; you merely have to call `TakePhotoAsync` or `PickPhotoAsync` to retrieve a `MediaFile` instance. Then, you can call `GetStream` to do what you want with the image data. In our case, we created `UIImage` to display directly in `UIImageView`. It is also necessary to use a `try-catch` block in case something unexpected happens or the user cancels.

You should now be able to run the app and select a photo to be viewed on the screen. The following screenshot shows a nice Xamarin logo that I selected from the photo library in my iOS simulator:

Accessing photos on Android

In comparison to iOS, we have to use a slightly different pattern on Android to retrieve photos from the camera or photo library. A common pattern in Android is it calls `StartActivityForResult` to launch an activity from another application. When this activity is completed, `OnActivityResult` will be called from your activity. Because of this, Xamarin.Mobile could not use the same APIs on Android as the other platforms. To start our example, create an Android Application project by going to **Android** | **Android Application** in Xamarin Studio. Make sure you add Xamarin.Mobile to the project from the Component Store.

Let's create two **Buttons** and an **ImageView** to mimic our UI on iOS as follows:

1. Open the `Main.axml` file from the `layout` folder under the `Resources` directory in the Android designer.

2. Remove the default button from the project template and add two new `Buttons` named `Library` and `Camera`.

3. Set their **Id** fields to `@+id/library` and `@+id/camera`, respectively.

4. Create an `ImageView` with **Id** of `@+id/imageView`.

5. Save the file and open `MainActivity.cs` so that we can make changes to our code.

As usual, remove any extra code that was created by the project template. Next, add a using statement for Xamarin.Media. Then, we can add a new OnCreate method and some member variables for our activity as follows:

```
MediaPicker picker;
ImageView imageView;
protected override void OnCreate(Bundle bundle)
{
  base.OnCreate(bundle);
  SetContentView(Resource.Layout.Main);
  var library = FindViewById<Button>(Resource.Id.library);
  var camera = FindViewById<Button>(Resource.Id.camera);
  imageView = FindViewById<ImageView>(Resource.Id.imageView);
  picker = new MediaPicker(this);
  library.Click += OnLibrary;
  camera.Click += OnCamera;
  if (!picker.IsCameraAvailable)
    camera.Enabled = false;
}
```

We retrieved the instance of our views and created a new MediaPicker by passing our activity as Context to its constructor. We hooked up some Click event handlers, and disabled the camera button since a camera is not available.

Next, let's implement the two Click event handlers as follows:

```
void OnLibrary (object sender, EventArgs e)
{
  var intent = picker.GetPickPhotoUI();
  StartActivityForResult (intent, 1);
}
void OnCamera (object sender, EventArgs e)
{
  var intent = picker.GetTakePhotoUI(new StoreCameraMediaOptions
  {
    Name = "test.jpg",
    Directory = "PhotoPicker"
  });
  StartActivityForResult (intent, 1);
}
```

In each case, we make a call to GetPickPhotoUI or GetTakePhotoUI in order to get an instance of an Android Intent object. This object is used to start new activities within an application. StartActivityForResult will also start the Intent object, expecting a result to be returned from the new activity. We also set some values with StoreCameraMediaOptions to specify a filename and temporary directory to store the photo.

Next, we need to implement `OnActivityResult` in order to handle what will happen when the new activity is completed:

```
protected async override void OnActivityResult(
  int requestCode, Result resultCode, Intent data)
{
  if (resultCode == Result.Canceled)
    return;
  var file = await data.GetMediaFileExtraAsync(this);
  using (var stream = file.GetStream())
  {
    imageView.SetImageBitmap(await
      BitmapFactory.DecodeStreamAsync(stream));
  }
}
```

If this is successful, we retrieve `MediaFile` and load `Bitmap` with the returned `Stream`. Next, all that is needed is to call `SetImageBitmap` to display the image on the screen.

You should now be able to run the application and load photos to be displayed on the screen as shown in the following screenshot:

Summary

In this chapter, we discovered the Xamarin.Mobile library and how it can accelerate common tasks in a cross-platform way. We retrieved contacts from the address book and set up GPS location updates over time. Lastly, we loaded photos from the camera and photo library.

After completing this chapter, you should have a complete grasp of the Xamarin. Mobile library and the common functionality it provides for cross-platform development. It provides clean, modern APIs that offer `async`/`await` functionality that can be accessed across iOS, Android, and Windows Phone. Accessing contacts, GPS, and photos across platforms is very straightforward with Xamarin.Mobile.

In the next chapter, we will cover the steps on how to submit applications to the iOS App Store and Google Play. This will include preparing your app to pass the iOS guidelines as well as properly signing up your app for Google Play.

11
App Store Submission

Now that you have completed the development of your cross-platform application, the next obvious step is to distribute your app on the app stores. Xamarin apps are distributed in exactly the same way as Java or Objective-C apps; however, there are still a lot of hoops to jump through to successfully get your applications in the stores. iOS has an official approval process, which makes app store submission a much more lengthier process than Android. Developers have to wait from a week, a month, or longer, depending on how many times the app is rejected. Android requires some additional steps to submit the app on Google Play compared to debugging your application, but you can still get your application submitted in just a few hours.

In this chapter, we will cover:

- The App Store Review Guidelines
- Submitting an iOS app to the App Store
- Setting up Android signing keys
- Submitting an Android app to Google Play
- Tips for being successful on app stores

Following the iOS App Store Review Guidelines

Your application's name, app icon, screenshots, and other aspects are declared on Apple's website called iTunes Connect. Sales reports, app store rejections, contract and bank information, and app updates are all managed through the website at `http://itunesconnect.apple.com`.

The primary purpose of Apple's guidelines is to keep the iOS App Store safe and free of malware. There is certainly little to no malware found on the iOS App Store.

Generally, the worst thing an iOS application could do to you is bombard you with ads. To a certain extent, the guidelines also reinforce Apple's revenue share with payments within your application. Sadly, some of Apple's guidelines controversially eliminate a competitor in a key area on iOS.

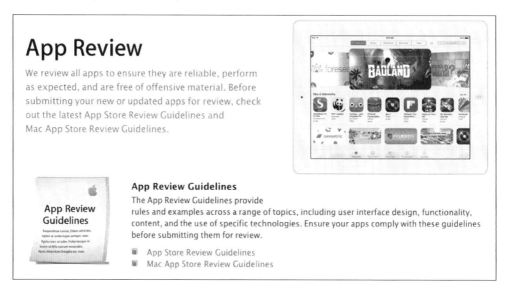

However, the key point here is to get your applications through the store approval process without facing App Store rejections. As long as you are not intentionally trying to break the rules, most applications will not face much difficulty in getting approved. The most common rejections are related to mistakes by developers, which is a good thing, since you would not want to release an app with a critical issue to the public.

The App Store Review Guidelines are quite lengthy, so let's break it down into the most common situations you might run into. A full list of the guidelines are found at `https://developer.apple.com/appstore/resources/approval/guidelines.html`. Note that a valid iOS developer account is required to view this site.

Some general rules to follow are:

- Applications that crash, have bugs, or fail critically will be rejected

- Applications that do not perform as advertised or contain hidden features will be rejected

- Applications that use non-public Apple APIs, or read/write files from prohibited locations on the filesystem will be rejected

- Apps that provide little value or that have been overdone (such as flashlight, burp, or fart apps) will be rejected

- Applications cannot use trademarked words as the app name or keywords without the permission of the trademark holder

- Applications cannot distribute copyrighted material illegally

- Apps that can simply be implemented by a mobile-friendly website, such as apps with lots of HTML content that provide no native functionality, can be rejected

These rules make sense to keep the overall quality and safety of the iOS App Store higher than it would have otherwise been. It can be difficult to get a simple app with very few features into the store due to some of these rules, so be sure that your app is useful and compelling enough for the App Store review team to allow it to be available on the store.

Some rules related to the mistakes made by developers or incorrect labeling in iTunes Connect are as follows:

- Applications or metadata that mention other mobile platforms such as Android, for example, will be rejected

- Applications that are labeled with an incorrect or inappropriate category/genre, screenshots, or icons will be rejected

- Developers must give an appropriate age rating and keywords for the application

- Support, privacy policy, and marketing URLs must be functional at the time the app is reviewed

- Developers should not declare iOS features that are not used; for example, do not declare Game Center or iCloud usage if your application does not actually use these features

- Applications that use features such as location or push notifications without the consent of the user will be rejected

These can sometimes simply be a mistake on the developer's part. Just make sure you double-check all of your application's information before that final submission to the iOS App Store.

Additionally, Apple has the following rules regarding content that can be contained within an application:

- Applications that contain objectionable content or content that may be considered rude will be rejected

- Applications that are designed to upset or disgust users will be rejected

- Applications that contain excessive imagery of violence will be rejected

- Applications that target a specific government, race, culture, or company as enemies will be rejected

- Applications with icons or screenshots that do not adhere to the four and above age rating may be rejected

The app store delivers apps to children and adults alike. Apple also supports an **over 17** age restriction on applications; however, this will seriously limit the number of potential users who can download your application. It's best to keep applications clean and appropriate for as many ages as possible.

The next category of rules listed as follows are related to Apple's 70/30 revenue share from the App Store:

- Applications that link to products or software sold on a website may be rejected.

- Apps using a payment mechanism other than iOS **in-app purchases** (**IAPs**) will be rejected.

- Applications that use IAPs for purchasing physical goods will be rejected.

- Apps can display digital content that is purchased outside the application as long as you cannot link to or purchase from within the app. All digital content purchased within the app must use IAPs.

These rules are easy to follow, as long as you are not trying to circumvent Apple's revenue share in the App Store. Always use IAPs for unlocking digital content within your applications.

Last but not least, the following bullet list contains some general tips related to App Store rejections:

- If your application requires a username and password, be sure to include credentials under the **Demo Account Information** section for the app review team to use.

- If your application contains IAPs or other features that the app review team must explicitly test, be sure to include instructions in **Review Notes** to reach the appropriate screen in your application.

- Schedule ahead! Don't let your product's app rejection ruin a deadline; plan at least a month into your schedule for app store approval.

- When in doubt, be as descriptive as possible in the **Review Notes** section of iTunes Connect.

If your application does get rejected, most of the time there is an easy resolution. Apple's review team will explicitly reference the guidelines if a rule is broken and will include the relevant crash logs and screenshots. If you can correct an issue without submitting a new build, you can respond to the app review team via the **Resolution Center** option in the iTunes Connect website. If you upload a new build, this will put your application at the end of the queue to be reviewed.

There are certainly more in-depth and specific rules for features in iOS, so make sure you have a look at the complete set of guidelines if you are thinking about doing something creative or out of the box with an iOS feature. As always, if you are unsure about a specific guideline, it is best to seek professional, legal advice on the matter. Calling Apple's support number will not shed any light on the subject, since its support personnel is not allowed to give advice related to the App Store Review Guidelines.

Submitting an app to the iOS App Store

Before we get started with submitting our application to the store, we need to review a short checklist to make sure you are ready to do so. It is a pain to reach a point in the process and realize you have something missing or haven't done something quite right. Additionally, there are a few requirements that will need to be met by a designer or the marketing team, which should not necessarily be left up to the developer.

Make sure you have done the following prior to beginning with the submission:

- Your application's `Info.plist` file is completely filled out. This includes splash screen images, app icons, app name, and other settings that need to be filled out for advanced features. Note that the app name here is what is displayed under the application icon. It can be differ from the App Store name, and unlike the App Store name, it does not have to be unique from all the other apps in the store.

- You have at least three names selected for your app on the App Store. A name may be unavailable even if it is not currently taken on the App Store, as it could have been previously taken by a developer for an app that was removed from the store for some reason.

- You have a large 1024 x 1024 app icon image. There isn't a need to include this file in the application, unless you are distributing enterprise or ad-hoc builds through iTunes (the desktop application).

- You have at least one screenshot per device that your application is targeting. This includes iPhone 4 retina, iPhone 5, and iPad retina sized screenshots for a universal iOS application. However, I would strongly recommend filling out all five screenshot slots.

- You have a well-written and edited description for the App Store.
- You have selected a set of keywords to improve the search results for your application.

Creating a distribution provisioning profile

Once you have double-checked the preceding checklist, we can begin the process for submission. Our first step will be to create a provisioning profile for App Store distribution.

Let's begin creating a new provisioning profile by carrying out the following steps:

1. Navigate to `http://developer.apple.com/ios`.
2. Click on **Certificates, Identifiers & Profiles** in the right-hand navigation bar.
3. Click on **Provisioning Profiles**.
4. Click on the plus button in the top-right corner of the window.
5. Select **App Store** under **Distribution** and click on **Continue**.
6. Select your app ID. You should have created one already in *Chapter 7, Deploying and Testing on Devices*; click on **Continue**.
7. Select the certificate for the provisioning profile. Normally, there will be only one option here. Click on **Continue**.
8. Give the profile an appropriate name such as `MyAppAppStore`. Click on **Generate**.
9. Once complete, you can download and install the profile manually or synchronize your provisioning profiles in Xcode under **Preferences | Accounts**, as we did earlier in the book.

You will arrive at the following screen when successful:

Download and Install

Download and double click the following file to install your Provisioning Profile.

Name:	XamChatAppStore
Type:	Distribution
App ID:	.com.jonathanpeppers.xamchat
Expires:	Nov 08, 2014

Download

Adding your app to iTunes Connect

For our next set of steps, we will start filling out the details of your application to be displayed on the Apple App Store.

We can begin by performing the following set of steps to set up your app in iTunes Connect:

1. Navigate to `http://itunesconnect.apple.com` and log in.

2. Click on **Manage Your Apps**.

3. Click on **Add New App** in the top-left corner of the window.

4. Enter an app name to be displayed on the App Store.

5. Enter a value in the **SKU Number** field. This is used to identify your app in reports.

6. In the **Bundle ID** field, enter the same bundle ID for which we just created a provisioning profile and click on **Continue**.

7. Select your app ID. You should have already created one in *Chapter 7, Deploying and Testing on Devices*; click on **Continue**.

8. Select inputs for your app's **Price Tier** and **Availability Date** fields and then click on **Continue**.

9. Fill out the **Version Number** and **Copyright** fields.

10. Select the primary and secondary **Category** options for your app.

11. Fill out the **Rating** information for your app.

12. Fill out your app's **Description**, **Keywords**, and **Support URL** fields.

13. Enter a value to the **App Review Contact Information** field. Leave out the information of the primary developer of the application.

14. Upload an icon using the **Large App Icon** and **Screenshots** options for each device your app supports.

15. Click on **Save**.

There are a lot of optional fields too. Make sure you fill out **Review Notes** or **Demo Account Information** if there is any additional information the app review team will require to review your application. When complete, you will see your application with the status **Prepare for Upload** as shown the in the following screenshot:

Now we need to notify iTunes Connect that we are ready to upload our application. Click on **View Details** and then on **Ready to Upload Binary**. You must then answer a few questions to comply with international export laws. The status of your application will then change to **Waiting for Upload**, and you'll receive a confirmation e-mail.

Making an iOS binary for the App Store

Our last step for App Store submission is to provide the binary file containing our application to the store. We need to create the **Release** build of our application, signed with the distribution provisioning profile we created earlier in this chapter.

Xamarin Studio makes this very simple. We can configure the build as follows:

1. Click on the solution configuration dropdown in the top-left corner of Xamarin Studio and select **AppStore**.

2. By default, Xamarin Studio will set all the configuration options that you need to submit this build configuration.

3. Next, select your iOS application project and click on **Build | Archive**.

After a few moments, Xamarin Studio will open the archived builds menu which looks like what is shown in the following screenshot:

The process creates a `xarchive` file that is stored in `~/Library/Developer/Xcode/Archives`. The **Validate...** button will check your archive for any potential errors that could occur during upload, while **Distribute...** will actually submit the application to the store. Sadly, at the time of writing this book, the **Distribute...** button merely launches the **Application Loader** application, which cannot upload `xarchive` files. Until Xamarin works this out, you can access these options from the archive in Xcode under **Window | Organizer** in the **Archives** tab.

Go ahead and locate the archive in Xcode; you may have to restart Xcode if it does not appear and perform the following steps:

1. Click on **Distribute...**. Don't worry, it will validate the archive before uploading.

2. Select **Submit to the iOS App Store** and click on **Next**.

3. Log in with your credentials for iTunes Connect and click on **Next**.

4. Select the appropriate provisioning profile for the application and click on **Submit**.

After several moments, depending on the size of your application, you will get a confirmation screen and the status of your application will change to **Upload Received**. The following screenshot shows what a confirmation screen looks like:

After a few minutes, you will receive an e-mail confirmation that the upload was received and the status of your application will change to **Waiting for Review**. At this point, you have no control on the status of your application while it's waiting in line to be reviewed by an Apple employee. This can take one to two weeks, depending on the current workload of apps to be reviewed and the time of year. Updates will also go through this same process, but the wait time is generally a bit shorter than a new app submission.

Luckily, there are a few situations where you can fast track this process. If you navigate to `https://developer.apple.com/appstore/contact/?topic=expedite`, you can request an expedited app review. Your issue must either be a critical bug fix or a time-sensitive event related to your application. Apple doesn't guarantee accepting an expedite request, but it can be a lifesaver in times of need.

Additionally, if something goes wrong with a build you submitted, you can cancel the submission by going to **Manage Your Apps** from the main dashboard, then selecting your application and clicking on **View Details** on the version you want to edit. Under **Version Information** | **Binary Details**, you can select **Reject this Binary** to cancel the submission. In situations where you discover a bug after submission, this allows you to upload a new build in its place. The following screenshot shows the binary file details:

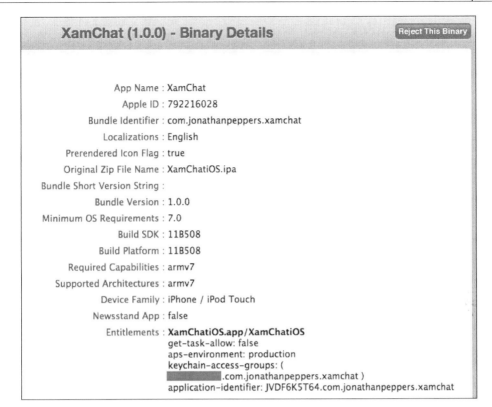

Signing your Android applications

All Android packages (apk files) are signed by a certificate or a keystore file to enable their installation on a device. When you are debugging/developing your application, your package is automatically signed by a development certificate that was generated by the Android SDK. It is fine to use this certificate for development or even beta testing; however, it cannot be used on an application distributed to Google Play.

To create a production certificate, we can use a command-line tool included with the Android SDK named keytool. To create your own keystore file, run the following line in a terminal window:

```
keytool -genkey -v -keystore <filename>.keystore -alias <key-name>
-keyalg RSA -keysize 2048 -validity 10000
```

Replace `<filename>` and `<key-name>` with appropriate terms for your application. The `keytool` command-line tool will then prompt several questions for you to identify the party that is signing the application. This is very similar to an **SSL** certificate, if you have ever worked with one before. You will also be prompted for a keystore password and a key password; you can let these be the same or change them, depending on how secure you want your key to be.

Your console output will look something like what is shown in the following screenshot:

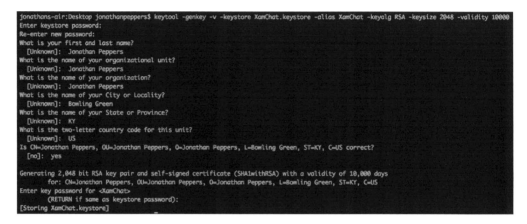

When complete, you should store your `keystore` file and password in a very safe place. Once you sign an application with this `keystore` file and submit it to Google Play, you will not be able to submit updates of the application without signing it with the same certificate. There is no mechanism to retrieve a lost `keystore` file. If you do happen to lose it, your only option is to remove the existing app from the store and submit a new app that contains your updated changes. This could potentially cause you to lose a lot of users.

To sign an Android package, you can use another command-line tool included with the Android SDK named `jarsigner`. However, Xamarin Studio simplifies this process by providing a user interface to run your package.

Open your Android project in Xamarin Studio and carry out the following steps to walk through the process of signing an `apk` file:

1. Change your build configuration to **Release**.
2. Select the appropriate project and navigate to **Project | Publish Android Application**.
3. Select the `keystore` file that you just created.

4. Enter values in the **Password**, **Alias**, and **Key Password** fields you used when creating the key. Click on **Forward**.

5. Choose a directory to deploy the `apk` file and click on **Create**.

When successful, a pad in Xamarin Studio will appear displaying the progress. The pad that appears looks like what is shown in the following screenshot:

```
Publishing package

Waiting for packaging to complete

Signing package with custom key

Package successfully signed
File created: /Users/jonathanpeppers/Desktop/com.jonathanpeppers.xamchat.apk
```

It is important to note that Xamarin.Android automatically runs a second tool called `zipalign` after signing the APK. This tool aligns the bytes within an APK to improve the startup time of your app. If you plan on running `jarsigner` from the command line itself, you must run `zipalign` as well. Otherwise, the app will crash on startup, and Google Play will also not accept the APK.

Submitting the app to Google Play

Once you have a signed Android package, submitting your application to Google Play is relatively painless compared to iOS. Everything can be completed via the **Developer Console** tab in the browser without having to upload the package with an OS X application.

Before starting the submission, make sure you have completed the tasks on the following checklist:

- You have declared an `AndroidManifest.xml` file with your application name, package name, and icon declared.
- You have an `apk` file signed with a production key.
- You have selected an application name for Google Play. This is not unique across the store.
- You have a 512 x 512 high-resolution icon image for Google Play.
- You have a well-written and edited description for the store.
- You have at least two screenshots. However, I recommend using all eight slots that include sizes for phones and 7-inch and 10-inch tablets.

After going through the checklist, you should be fully prepared to submit your application to Google Play. The tab for adding new apps looks like the following screenshot:

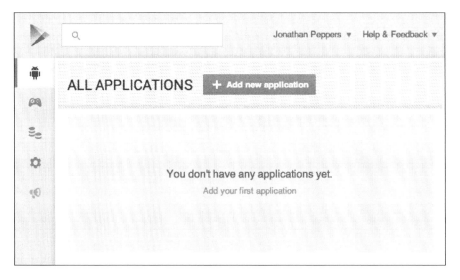

To begin with, navigate to `https://play.google.com/apps/publish` and log in to your account and carry out the following steps:

1. Select the **All Applications** tab and click on **Add new application**.

2. Enter a name to be displayed for the app on Google Play and click on **Upload APK**.

3. Click on **Upload your first APK to Production**.

4. Browse to your signed `apk` file and click on **OK**. You will see the **APK** tab's checkmark turn green.

5. Select the **Store Listing** tab.

6. Fill out all the required fields including **Description**, **High-res Icon**, **Categorization**, and **Privacy Policy** (or select the checkbox saying you aren't submitting a policy), and provide at least two screenshots.

7. Click on **Save**. You will see the checkmark on the **Store Listing** tab turn green.

8. Select the **Pricing & Distribution** tab.

9. Select a price and the countries you wish to distribute to.

10. Accept the agreement for **Content guidelines** and **US export laws**.

11. Click on **Save**. You will see the checkmark on the **Pricing & Distribution** tab turn green.

12. Select the **Ready to publish** dropdown in the top-right corner as shown in the following screenshot, and select **Publish this app**:

In a few hours, your application will be available on Google Play. No approval process is required, and updates to your apps are equally painless.

Google Play Developer Program Policies

To provide a safe store environment, Google retroactively removes applications that violate its policies and will generally ban the entire developer account—not just the application. Google's policies are are aimed at improving the quality of applications available on Google Play and are not quite as lengthy as the set of rules on iOS. That being said, the following is a basic summary of Google's policies:

- Apps cannot have sexually explicit material, gratuitous violence, or hate speeches.

- Apps cannot infringe upon copyrighted material.

- Apps cannot be malicious in nature, or capture private information of users without their knowledge.

- Apps cannot modify the basic functionalities of users' devices (such as modifying the home screen) without their consent. If applications include this functionality, it must be easy for users to turn off this functionality.

- All digital content within your application must use Google Play's in-app billing (or in-app purchases). Physical goods cannot be purchased with IAPs.

- Applications must not abuse cellular network usage that could result in the user incurring high bill amounts.

As with iOS, if you have a concern about one of the policies, it is best to procure professional, legal advice about the policy. For a complete list of the policies, visit `https://play.google.com/about/developer-content-policy.html`.

Google Play Developer Program Policies

The policies listed below play an important role in maintaining a positive experience for everyone using Google Play. Defined terms used here have the same meaning as in the Developer Distribution Agreement. Be sure to check back from time to time, as these policies may change.

Content Policies

Our content policies apply to any content your app displays or links to, including any ads it shows to users and any user-generated content it hosts or links to. Further, they apply to any content from your developer account which is publicly displayed in Google Play, including your developer name and the landing page of your listed developer website. In addition to complying with these policies, the content of your app must be rated in accordance with our Content Rating Guidelines.

Tips for a successful mobile app

From my personal experience, I have been submitting applications built with Xamarin to the iOS App Store and Google Play for quite some time. After delivering nearly 40 mobile applications totaling ten million downloads, a lot of lessons are to be learned about what makes a mobile application successful or a failure. Xamarin apps are indistinguishable from Java or Objective-C apps to the end user, so you can make your app successful by following the same patterns as standard iOS or Android applications.

There is quite a bit you can do to make your app more successful. The following list contains some tips to follow:

- **Pricing it right**: If your application appeals to everyone and everywhere, consider a **freemium** model that makes revenue from ad placements or in-app purchases. However, if your app is fairly niche, you will be much better off pricing your app at $1.99 or higher. Premium apps must also hold a higher standard of quality.

- **Knowing your competition**: If there are other apps in the same space as yours, make sure your application is better or offers a much wider feature set than the competition. It might also be a good idea to avoid the space altogether if there are already several apps with the same functionalities as yours.

- **Prompting loyal users for reviews**: It is a good idea to prompt users for a review after they open your application several times. This gives users, who really like your application a chance to write a good review.

- **Supporting your users**: Provide a valid support e-mail address or Facebook page for you to easily interact with your users. Respond to bug reports and negative reviews—Google Play even has the option to e-mail users who write reviews on your app.

- **Keeping your application small**: Staying under the 100 MB limit on iOS or 50 MB on Google Play will allow users to download your application on their cellular data plan. Doing this negates the possibility of friction to install your app as users will associate a lengthy download with a slow running application.

- **Submitting your app to review websites**: Try to get as many reviews on the Web as possible. Apple provides the ability to send coupon codes, but with the Android version of your app, you could send your actual Android package. Sending your app to review websites or popular YouTube channels can be a great way to free advertising.

- **Using an app analytics or tracking service**: Reporting your app's usage and crash reports can be very helpful to understand your users. Fixing crashes in the wild and modifying your user interface to improve spending behavior is very important.

There is no silver bullet to having a successful mobile application. If your application is compelling, fulfills a need, and functions quickly and properly, you could have the next hit on your hands. Being able to deliver a consistent cross-platform experience using Xamarin will also give you a head start on your competitors.

Summary

In this chapter, we covered everything you need to know to submit your application to the iOS App Store and Google Play. We covered the App Store Review Guidelines and simplified them for the most common situations you might run into during the approval process. We went over the set up process for provisioning your app's metadata and uploading your binary to iTunes Connect. For Android, we went over how to create a production signing key and sign your Android package (apk) file. We went over submitting an application to Google Play, and finished the chapter with tips on delivering a successfully and hopefully profitable application to the app stores.

I hope that with this book, you have experienced an end-to-end, practical walkthrough for developing real-world, cross-platform applications with Xamarin. Using C#, which is such a great language compared to the alternatives, you should be very productive. Additionally, you will save time by sharing code without, in any way, limiting the native experience for your users.

Index

await keyword 203
Azure Account
  setting up 155, 156
Azure Mobile Services
  about 153, 154
  data types. updating for 162
  exploring 157, 158
  features 157
Azure websites 154

B

backend
  adding, to XamChat 161
backend, adding to XamChat
  data types, updating for Azure Mobile
      Services 162
  Xamarin component, using 163-169
banking
  setting up, for Google Merchant Account 16
BaseAdapter
  using 118-120
Base Class Libraries (BCL) 21
basics, iOS app 81-83
blob storage 154
bundle ID
  creating 136

C

camera
  accessing 216, 217
categories, segue
  custom 92
  modal 92
  push 92
  relationship 92
certificate signing request
  setting up 172
C# libraries
  porting 187-190
cloned project files 43
Cloud services 154
common services, Windows Azure
  Cloud services 154
  mobile services 154
  service bus 154
  SQL Azure 154

  storage 154
  virtual machines 154
  websites 154
  worker roles 154
components, Xamarin
  ActionBarSherlock 186
  Facebook SDK 186
  Json.NET 186
  RestSharp 186
  SQLite.NET 186
  Xamarin.Mobile 186
contacts
  accessing 205-207
  retrieving, on Android 208, 209
controller
  adding, to application 26, 27
CoreGraphics 191
crash 152
cross-platform solutions
  setting up 47
cross-platform solutions, options
  cloned project files 43
  file linking 43
  portable class libraries 44

D

data binding 39
datatypes
  updating, for Azure Mobile Services 162
dependency injection
  about 44, 51
  simplifying 51-53
DidEnterBackground method 28
distribution provisioning profile
  creating 228
dynamic schema 158

E

editions, Xamarin
  Business edition 10
  Enterprise edition 10
  Indie edition 9
  Starter edition 9

Thank you for buying
Xamarin Cross-platform Application Development

About Packt Publishing

Packt, pronounced 'packed', published its first book "*Mastering phpMyAdmin for Effective MySQL Management*" in April 2004 and subsequently continued to specialize in publishing highly focused books on specific technologies and solutions.

Our books and publications share the experiences of your fellow IT professionals in adapting and customizing today's systems, applications, and frameworks. Our solution based books give you the knowledge and power to customize the software and technologies you're using to get the job done. Packt books are more specific and less general than the IT books you have seen in the past. Our unique business model allows us to bring you more focused information, giving you more of what you need to know, and less of what you don't.

Packt is a modern, yet unique publishing company, which focuses on producing quality, cutting-edge books for communities of developers, administrators, and newbies alike. For more information, please visit our website: `www.packtpub.com`.

Writing for Packt

We welcome all inquiries from people who are interested in authoring. Book proposals should be sent to `author@packtpub.com`. If your book idea is still at an early stage and you would like to discuss it first before writing a formal book proposal, contact us; one of our commissioning editors will get in touch with you.

We're not just looking for published authors; if you have strong technical skills but no writing experience, our experienced editors can help you develop a writing career, or simply get some additional reward for your expertise.

Appcelerator Titanium Business Application Development Cookbook

ISBN: 978-1-84969-534-3   Paperback: 328 pages

Over 40 hands-on recipes to quickly and efficiently create business grade Titanium Enterprise apps

1. Provide mobile solutions to meet the challenges of today's Enterprise mobility needs.

2. Study the best practices in security, document management, and Titanium Enterprise Development.

3. Create cross-platform Enterprise class Titanium apps quickly and efficiently with step-by-step instructions and images to help guide you.

Android Studio Application Development

ISBN: 978-1-78328-527-3   Paperback: 110 pages

Create visually appealing applications using the new IntelliJ IDE Android Studio

1. Familiarize yourself with Android Studio IDE.

2. Enhance the user interface for your app using the graphical editor feature.

3. Explore the various features involved in developing an Android app and implement them.

Please check **www.PacktPub.com** for information on our titles

Made in the USA
San Bernardino, CA
28 May 2014